The Secret Reasons Why Teachers Are Not Using Web 2.0 Tools and What School Librarians Can Do about It

The Secret Reasons Why Teachers Are Not Using Web 2.0 Tools and What School Librarians Can Do about It

Peggy Milam Creighton

AN IMPRINT OF ABC-CLIO, LLC
Santa Barbara, California • Denver, Colorado • Oxford, England

Copyright 2012 by ABC-CLIO, LLC

All rights reserved. No part of this publication may be reproduced, stored in a retrieval system, or transmitted, in any form or by any means, electronic, mechanical, photocopying, recording, or otherwise, except for the inclusion of brief quotations in a review, or reproducibles, which may be copied for classroom and educational programs only, without prior permission in writing from the publisher.

Library of Congress Cataloging-in-Publication Data

Creighton, Peggy Milam.

  The secret reasons why teachers are not using web 2.0 tools and what school librarians can do about it / Peggy Milam Creighton.

       p. cm.

   Includes index.

   ISBN 978-1-58683-532-3 (pbk.) — ISBN 978-1-58683-533-0 (ebook)   1. Internet in education.   2. School libraries—Computer network resources.   3. Web 2.0.   I. Title.

   LB1044.87.C754   2012

   371.33'44678—dc23   2011051501

ISBN: 978-1-58683-532-3
EISBN: 978-1-58683-533-0

16 15 14 13 12   1 2 3 4 5

This book is also available on the World Wide Web as an eBook.
Visit www.abc-clio.com for details.

Linworth
An Imprint of ABC-CLIO, LLC

ABC-CLIO, LLC
130 Cremona Drive, P.O. Box 1911
Santa Barbara, California 93116-1911

This book is printed on acid-free paper ∞

Manufactured in the United States of America

This book is dedicated to
Vern, Ryan, and Kristen,
who are always in my heart.

Contents

Acknowledgments ix
Introduction xi

CHAPTER 1: What Is Web 2.0? 1
    What Do You Know about Web 2.0?. 1
    Defining the World Wide Web 2
    Defining Web 2.0 6
    Web 2.0 Teaching Tools to Use Now!. 21
    Where Do We Go from Here?. 31
    Action Steps 32
    Interactive Features of This Chapter. 32
    Final Thoughts 33
    Extending the Conversation 33

CHAPTER 2: Barriers to Using Web 2.0 in 21st-Century Schools 37
    The Impact of Web 2.0 on K–12 Education 38
    The Digital Divide. 45
    Advantages of Web 2.0 49
    Disadvantages of Web 2.0. 51
    Action Steps 53
    Extending the Conversation 53

CHAPTER 3: School Library 2.0 55

    Web 2.0 56
    Web 2.0 Tools for School Librarians and Readers to Use Now! 58
    Other Popular Tools 68
    Implications for School Librarians 72
    Action Steps 72
    Final Thoughts 73
    Extending the Conversation 73

CHAPTER 4: Interpreting the Research 75

    Research on Web 2.0 in 21st-Century Schools 76
    Research-based Reasons Teachers Are Not Using Web 2.0 76
    Implications for Practice 83
    Action Steps 84
    Extending the Conversation 84

CHAPTER 5: How School Librarians Can Serve as
Change Agents in Their Schools 87

    The Setting 88
    The Seven-Step Plan 89
    Scenarios 91
    Influence Beyond the Local School 93
    Next Steps 99
    Extending the Conversation 99

Glossary 101
Works Cited 105
Index 109

Acknowledgments

I would like to thank Blanche Woolls for her editing expertise and guidance in completing this project. I would also like to thank my husband, Vern, for his patience and support while I worked late hours completing this manuscript. Without his unflinching belief in me, I could not have finished this project on time. I would also like to thank my children, Ryan and Kristen, who are my biggest cheerleaders.

Introduction

My favorite aunt has more Facebook friends than I do. She creates photo streams and links to videos and even sends me e-cards on special occasions. Although she is 80-something, she connects to social networks from her smart phone and computer. She has joined the technology revolution (Braulein, 2008).

Web 2.0 has brought about this technology revolution. What is Web 2.0? According to Will Richardson (2010), Web 2.0 is the read-write web; it is a community of users who can collaboratively post text, images, and other multimedia, while all of the connected world can respond online to these postings.

Web 2.0 is responsible for the rapid growth of interactive digital tools for creating, communicating, and collaborating online. Commerce, medicine, transportation, the military, and other industries quickly adapted to the techno-revolution, creating Facebook pages and Tweeting, posting to blogs and subscribing to RSS feeds, soliciting customer ratings and comments, and creating a real-time online presence. The education industry, however, has lagged far behind. As a result, today's high school graduates are not well prepared to enter a digital workforce.

Substantial efforts have been made to bring schools into the 21st-century connected world, which has produced a plan to help schools go digital, according to Braulein (2008). School districts across the country are spending record amounts on 21st-century tools such as interactive white boards, ceiling-mounted projectors, and student response systems, but are they being used? Unfortunately, research indicates that technology integration has not reached its full potential and that teachers lament about lack of time, lack of technology training, lack of administrative support for technology integration efforts, lack of opportunity to practice skills, and other barriers to use (Creighton, 2010). In some schools, teachers are still not integrating technology into instruction, and are not using Web 2.0 tools at all.

In view of this situation, what can school librarians do? There has never been a greater need for practicing school librarians to get involved. I see the present time as a wake-up call for school library media specialists to become vocal social change agents, vociferous advocates for school library programs, and voracious consumers of Web 2.0 tools. It is a time when school librarians, who already wear many hats, should add yet one more—a Library 2.0 trainer hat.

Although some school librarians think they should stick to only what is written in their job descriptions, it may be time to reconsider. While budget cuts have struck many from the faculty list, school librarians can reposition themselves as the most important member of the faculty and add an extra layer of job security to their positions. By leveraging leadership, collaboration, and technology skills they already possess in their repertoire, school librarians can evolve into media experts as well as critical partners. They can meet the needs of 21st-century learners and add to their resumés at the same time. They can tweak their influence to effect positive social change in their schools and districts.

The purpose of this book is to detail the current state of technology integration and Internet use in K–12 schools, and the reasons why classroom teachers often fail to incorporate Web 2.0 tools into their instruction and collaboration with other educators. The book will cover authoritative definitions of Web 2.0, the types of Web 2.0 tools suited for use in educational settings, the research-based reasons they are underutilized, and strategies for school librarians to model their use and teach others to do so, as well.

Written in simple terms, this book will appeal to school librarians, practicing K–12 educators, K–12 school and district administrators, teacher educators, and researchers in the field of K–12 education who wish to effect a positive social change in improving student achievement.

CHAPTER 1

What Is Web 2.0?

This chapter will take a fresh look at Web 2.0, the read-write web, from the perspective of current authorities in the educational field. It will include examples of wikis, blogs, digital storytelling, document sharing, podcasts, vodcasts, instant messaging, photo streams, resource sharing, social mapping, and more. Subtopics include:

- Current definitions from authoritative sources
- Examples of Web 2.0 tools
- Samples of Web 2.0 tools for K–12 education
- Screenshots and links

Although this chapter will begin with a definition of the World Wide Web that you may not need, teachers with whom you work may need some additional explanation. So what do you know about Web 2.0?

What Do You Know about Web 2.0?

Even though you might use the World Wide Web on a regular basis and might think you know all about it, Web 2.0 represents a change in online activities and services, and, consequently, a change in the mindset of users.

- Are you familiar with the difference between Web 2.0 and its predecessor?

- Do you know how the new World Wide Web came to be?
- Can you speak confidently to your students and faculty about the features of Web 2.0?
- Do you know which Web 2.0 sites are best for instructional purposes?

If not, read on! This chapter is just for you.

Defining the World Wide Web

The World Wide Web, abbreviated as WWW, is the group of networked interfaces and hypertext links that comprise the Internet. These networked links consist of web sites or pages that may contain images, text, videos, or multimedia. In order to retrieve these resources, Internet users must access the Internet through a web browser such as Internet Explorer, Mozilla/Firefox, or Google Chrome. Internet users will then use a search engine such as Bing (www.bing.com) or Google (www.google.com) to enter a key word or type in a URL (Universal Resource Locator) address such as www.myhomepage.org.

Reprinted with permission of the World Wide Web Consortium, 2011

The World Wide Web organization of the Internet has been attributed to Sir Tim Berners-Lee of the World Wide Web Consortium (W3C), who proposed a hypertext system in 1989 that formed the basis for the World Wide Web today. WWW users could browse for a website or go directly to it and then point and click to navigate through the content on the site. The technology of hyperlinking allowed web browsers to find multiple interrelated web sites containing similar content. Over time, two different approaches to searching developed: ad-free Netscape and ad-sponsored Google.

TIP

Read more about the history of the World Wide Web at: http://www.w3.org.

Netscape

As published on their website at http://www.mozilla.org/about/history.html, Netscape was the first browser to become Open Source, or to provide programming code freely to the public. Netscape's open source platform was named Mozilla, and was founded as a public service to make searching the web safer. Mozilla avoids the ads used in Google and provides a means of secure searching as well as additional safety plug-ins. Ad-free searching means that teachers and students will not be distracted by sometimes inappropriate advertising while trying to perform a search. Mozilla later morphed to Firefox, with the same public service philosophy and ad-free safety features. Read more about the Mozilla/Firefox protected browsing features at: www.mozilla.com/en-US/firefox/security/#philosophy.

Google Chrome

Google Chrome is a web browser created by Google Labs. Google Labs began with the search engine for which it is named—Google—designed by two Stanford graduate students, Larry Page and Sergey Brin. They collaborated on the design of a search engine they dubbed "BackRub," which initially ran on the Stanford servers. In 1997, they changed its name to Google, a play on the word "googol," and referring to the seemingly infinite amount of information on the World Wide Web. Their mission was to organize this information for a method of fast and efficient searching and retrieving of information. Google went public in 1998 and introduced their AdWords technology in 2000. Since that time, Google has continued to develop new and innovative strategies to capitalize on the interests of the public, adding image searching and APIs (application programming interfaces), which ensure that users see the same results when viewing web pages, with many new APIs constantly in development in Google Labs. Google also sought to go Open Source, with the introduction of it own web browser, Google Chrome.

Internet Explorer

Internet Explorer comes already installed as the default Internet browser on all Microsoft operating systems. Internet Explorer offers many customizable features and security options and works well with multiple search engines. Recently, the Microsoft Corporation, developer of the Internet Explorer browser, introduced its new search engine, Bing. A replacement for its less-successful Windows Live Search and MSN search, Bing sought to recover a share of the Google market, as well as utilize the profit-making features of Google through its Microsoft adCenter. Bing operates on a philosophy similar to that of Google, capitalizing on the search terms of its users to target advertising and corporate sponsors.

Safari

Although not cornering a larger portion of the web searching market, Apple's Safari web browser was once designed exclusively for Mac users, but now works with Windows operating systems, as well. Fast and efficient, this browser has many features that compare favorably with Google Chrome, but is not easily customizable and lacks the phishing protection and extra security features of Mozilla/Firefox. It does, however, perform well because it is sleek and less memory-intensive than its more popular competitors. Safari comes with a built-in default search engine.

Table 1.1: Comparison of Firefox, Google Chrome, Internet Explorer, and Safari Browsers

Firefox	Google Chrome	Internet Explorer	Safari
Netscape/Mozilla/Firefox philosophy: nonprofit organization believing in potential of the Internet to enrich others' lives rather than benefiting shareholders.	Google Chrome/Google philosophy: For-profit organization believing in a shared information philosophy; works on democracy principle and page rank algorithm, where it collects personal information to make searching more meaningful.	Internet Explorer/Bing Philosophy: For-profit alternative search strategy that organizes information into categories; provides general decision-making information on each search term.	Safari philosophy: Maintain the Apple reputation for excellence, aesthetics, and innovation with rich graphic display.
Open source	Google Chrome is open source (standard Google search engine is not)	Not open source	Not open source
Avoids ads	Sponsors ads, especially as pop-ups and sidebars	Sponsors ads, especially as sidebars and pop-ups	Sponsors ads as both pop-ups and sidebars
Custom settings	Personal settings option	Personal settings and advanced capabilities with Silverlight installation	Personal settings, bookmarks, and tabs; private browsing feature
Safety: antivirus/phishing/malware built-in	Safety is a concern of all; report unsafe occurrences	Safety features available with installed Bing tool bar	Safety is indicated by the small padlock in the upper right-side screen; extensions allow additional safety features
Plug-ins include private browsing, clear history, do not track, content security	Ad words/ad sense built-in components of operation	SERP, Queries table, traffic tabs in webmaster tool package	Limited extensions can clear private data, block profanity or domains, and manage passwords
Free download	Free download	Online with free download for Silverlight	Free download
Small percentage of users	Majority of users	Small but growing percentage of users	Apple/Mac users and a small percentage of Windows users

From *The Secret Reasons Why Teachers Are Not Using Web 2.0 Tools and What School Librarians Can Do about It* by Peggy Milam Creighton. Santa Barbara, CA : Libraries Unlimited. Copyright © 2012.

READER SURVEY 1

Which web browser do you use? Do you use Google Chrome, Internet Explorer, Safari, or Firefox? Log on to: http://secretreasons.wikispaces.com/Reader+Survey+1, and enter your responses to Survey 1. While there, you can see how others have voted!

There are multiple browsers on the market today, but Firefox, Chrome, and Internet Explorer stand out in terms of features and usage (see Table 1.1). It is the innovative strategies like Google's response to the interests of the public that propelled the static web into the interactive, collaborative, and constructivist web of today. This new social web has been dubbed Web 2.0.

Defining Web 2.0

Web 2.0 is a participatory web. While Web 1.0 contained read-only content, Web 2.0 allows users to read as well as to post new content. Victoria Shannon (2006) of the *New York Times* claimed that Web 2.0 means an Internet that is more user-centered, interactive, and commercialized than was the Internet 10 years ago. Unlike its predecessor, Web 2.0 is a two-way web. Content of Web 2.0 sites is not only owner-driven, but also socially and globally driven. Web 2.0 is an interactive web, allowing users to interact with posters of information and with each other. This connectivity, collaboration, and interactivity of Web 2.0 not only increase visits to and time spent on sites, but also spurs user activity and new content creation.

TIP

For more of Shannon's ideas about Web 2.0, visit: www.nytimes.com/2006/05/23/technology/23iht-web.html.

How Web 2.0 Differs from Web 1.0

The original World Wide Web contained static web pages. Static pages displayed content accessible by web browsers. These sites were static because the owner or site developer was solely responsible for the content that appeared on the site, which could include text, images, multimedia, and links. Once created, sites might remain unchanged indefinitely or were updated in accordance with the owner's wishes. This static system grew for approximately 15 years, until a major innovation brought about the advent of what is now called Web 2.0.

According to Will Richardson (2006), Web 2.0 is distinguished from Web 1.0 by its capacity for reading and writing to sites. This means that Web 2.0 is a socially constructed platform. Internet users can do more than simply access content. They can post comments to blogs and Facebook pages, tag content with informal keywords that help users locate material, collaborate with other Internet users in instant messaging (IM) and video chats, and create new content by uploading responses to blog posts and adding related photos, videos, audio files, and other multimedia. This interactive feature is what differentiates Web 2.0 from the original static Web 1.0. Advanced web programming languages (such as Ajax and Java) and greater bandwidth speeds have allowed increased user access as well as media-rich activity on sites.

Teachers in some schools saw potential in utilizing the World Wide Web for educational activities. As the number of users online grew, so did the number of schools and educators who maintained a website. Today, posting lesson plans, sharing projects, and assessing work online is a common educational practice. Schools have successfully

Creighton, 2011

Table 1.2: Comparison of Web 1.0 and Web 2.0

Web 1.0	Web 2.0
Dial-up	Broadband
Single-tasking	Multitasking
HTML	Ajax
Hard-wired	WiFi
E-mail	Social networking
Attachments	Stream/share an album
Static code	Dynamic code
Read-only content	Write content
Browsing	Collaborating
One-way	Two-way
Download from	Upload to
No user editing	Open editing
	Users comment, tag, upload, link, rate, create
Individual search	Multiple RSS feeds
Double-click advertising	Adsense, pop-ups, sidebars
Taxonomy	Folksonomy
Source-driven	Globally driven

From *The Secret Reasons Why Teachers Are Not Using Web 2.0 Tools and What School Librarians Can Do about It* by Peggy Milam Creighton. Santa Barbara, CA : Libraries Unlimited. Copyright © 2012.

> **TIP**
>
> Visit Will Richardson's blog to read some posts such as "Our 'Leaders' Are Illiterate," "Another School I'd Want for My Kids," "Why the Tests Don't Work," and learn more about Web 2.0 in education at: http://willrichardson.com/.

leveraged the power of communicating with other schools and students, interviewing authors, scientists, researchers, and other experts online, participating in webinars and virtual tours, inviting the world into their classrooms through webcams, and more.

Of course, there are some people who believe there is no difference between what is now known as Web 1.0 and Web 2.0. Some programmers claim that both versions of the web offered essentially the same products, services, and interactions, although with some improvements in the latest versions, of course. Both iterations of the web have offered a networked interface with email, text, images, search engines, browser navigation, hyperlinks, advertising, and more. Both iterations of the web have offered commercial sites as a common web-based practice, along with online publishing. Both iterations of the web have seen a rapid growth in personal as well as commercial websites as more and more users became connected. The major difference between Web 1.0 and Web 2.0, based on this argument, was in the number of users who were online at any given time and the types of interactions they conducted while online (see Figure 1.1 and Table 1.2).

Despite their similarities, the read-write web, or Web 2.0, has some specific features that make it different from Web 1.0, such as:

- collaboration
- social networking
- dynamic code
- cloud computing
- syndication
- folksonomies
- media sharing

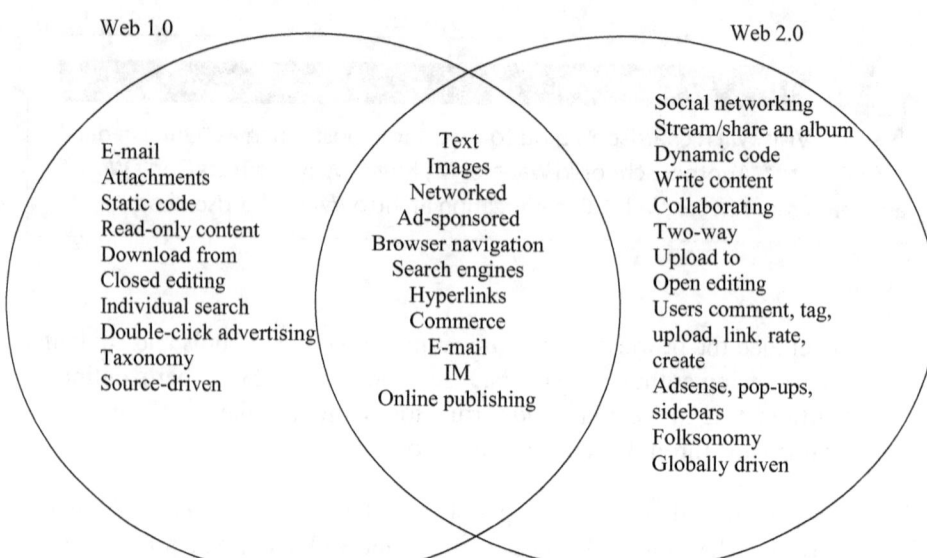

Figure 1.1: Commonalities between Web 1.0 and Web 2.0

Collaboration

The interactive, socially constructed Web 2.0 platform is responsible for a 21st-century phenomenon of user collaboration. Collaboration refers to the process of exchanging ideas and information for a common purpose. Collaboration may be as simple as posting the answer to a question, or as complex as co-authoring a book or a song. Collaboration online can be quite different from face-to-face collaboration, as Internet users not only share ideas with each other, but also interact with the content by commenting, tagging, sharing ideas, linking to similar or opposing content, and mixing, mashing up, and creating new content. Such collaboration makes the Web 2.0 content dynamic and client-based. The content of sites is constantly changing as Internet users visit and interact. Internet users create traffic that results in additional traffic and, thus, creates value for the owner of sites.

As users participate in commenting and sharing ideas, site designers benefit by gleaning suggestions for improving the site. In fact, when programming code is made freely available to all through open sourcing, Internet users themselves can help tweak the code to make it even more functional and efficient. Internet users can also make suggestions that programmers can evaluate to make their sites more user friendly.

Creighton, 2011

Client participation generates traffic on a site, which in turn, creates additional value for the owner. As site owners and designers make their sites content-rich, Internet users also benefit from the media available there. Sharing and tagging content with others has become wildly popular—or viral, as the jargon goes—as a feature of Web 2.0 known as social networking.

Social Networking

Social networking is the act of sharing information and media online with a group of other like-minded individuals, generally on a specific site. Internet users visit a site of interest and become members of that site to find others with similar interests. For example, users join Facebook to locate friends, post their profile, and share information with each other. They can post photos, links to sites of interest, share news and activities, play games, and more.

Social networking in schools is emerging as a means of posting to blogs; commenting on other blog posts; connecting with experts, organizations, and others with similar interests through sites such as Facebook; sharing resources through tweets; sharing media through sites such as YouTube; and more. Savvy school librarians can leverage the power of social networking by using blogs, microblogs, Facebook pages, and other social networking resources to connect to their student patrons and promoting their use to locate library resources. Although many social networking sites are blocked in schools to protect student safety, students are adept are navigating around blocks by accessing sites through their smartphones and other WiFi mobile devices or logging in off campus.

Social networking sites not only benefit from the Internet users who become members of their site, but they also benefit from the input those Internet users give to site content. Client activity on a site can increase the value of the site to others through tagging content, commenting on content, subscribing to RSS feeds that update them when new content is posted, and frequently posting their own content on a site. When Internet users post comments or link to their own sites and share these finds with others, their friends are updated on this activity, and new client activity is generated. Each new action creates an explosion of user activity from others as a result of Web 2.0

coding that makes sites interactive and dynamic. One of the early and wildly popular sites using social networking such as this is YouTube. This social networking site has become the standard online business platform and is characterized by its dynamic code.

READER SURVEY 2

Go to http://secretreasons.wikispaces.com/Reader+Survey+2 to respond to this survey.

- Do you use YouTube or some other media hosting site?
- Do you use Twitter or some other microblogging site?
- Do you use Library Thing or some other book cataloging site?
- Do you use Delicious or some other social bookmarking site?
- Do you have a Facebook or some other social networking page?
- Are such tools open to students or blocked in your district?

Dynamic Code

The first web sites to be posted online contained text and images that remained constant until the author uploaded new content. Uploads could be posted daily, as in a news or weather site, or could be updated once a month, once a year, or not at all. Such sites that change only at the author's command are static sites. Static sites were developed through the use of Hypertext Markup Language (HTML) that showed the same content to all viewers. Frequently, such sites were developed offline in a software development program and then uploaded through a File Transfer Protocol (FTP) that moved the code to a server that hosted a site.

Dynamic websites, on the other hand, are sites that are generated the moment a user accesses a URL. Web 2.0 technologies have allowed for websites to be coded so that the content changes continuously based on the user's activity. For example, when a client searches for weather in Detroit, dynamically coded sidebars may include other Detroit-related information, especially if the user has a search history that includes searches for restaurants, hotels, movies, parks, or other local attractions. Similarly, pop-ups may hover over a site while content is loading and may include user-centric advertising based on previous user activity or weather-related goods and services.

Dynamic sites use tools such as client-side or server-side scripting, cookies, and web analytics to track user activity and post appropriate pop-ups and sidebar advertising. Client-side scripting refers to code that activates sidebars and pop-up windows on the user side. Server-side scripting refers to coding that activates sidebar or pop-up windows from a server. Wherever the code is activated, it is the dynamic functionality that separates Web 2.0 from the original static html code of Web 1.0. Widgets, or small stand-alone applications that can be embedded on a site, take advantage of dynamic code to generate user-centric content.

READER SURVEY 3

What do you think of Google AdWords? Do you have any widgets embedded on your own blog or website?

Go to http://secretreasons.wikispaces.com/Reader+Survey+3 to respond to this survey.

Cloud Computing

A significant distinguishing feature of Web 2.0 is that applications reside on networked servers rather than on individual desktops. Accessing applications housed on networked servers is known as "cloud computing." Through cloud computing, Internet users no longer need to download programs in order to use them. Rather, they create an account, which is often free, and then make use of the application. The products they create with the application can be safely stored online and shared, linked, embedded, or downloaded for personal use. Sharing the products with friends or the general public allows others to benefit from them, and perhaps even tweak them for their own use. The result is that users' shared products have a chance to be improved by the input of others.

Creighton, 2011

For example, in order to perform word processing tasks, computer users originally needed to install a word processing software program onto their hard drives. Popular products included Microsoft Works or Word, or Corel. Disk space became an issue as Internet users saved an extensive library of documents or media to their hard drives. Over time, this became a problem, as storing consumed a lot of disk space. Original solutions to this problem included increasing hard drive space, saving to an external networked server, or saving to a backup tape drive, CD, or flash drive. As the cost of memory decreased, servers became larger and networked server space became an inexpensive viable option. With the advent of cloud computing, Internet users could then create and save their documents to a secure online server. Microsoft's Open Office provides an online version of Word, PowerPoint, Publisher, Excel, or Access for such a purpose.

The advantage of cloud computing is its ubiquity, or constant availability. Documents are available anytime, anywhere, from any computer with Internet access. Internet users no longer have to make multiple copies of documents and move them around on portable storage devices. For presentations at staff meetings and educational conferences, Internet users simply need Internet access to retrieve their presentations.

In addition, Internet users can share their work with others by designating which documents are public and which are private, as well as who can obtain access to their documents online and what level of access they have: view only or edit. Cloud computing is the green solution of the 21st century. It allows 24/7 access to documents for editing purposes, allows documents to be shared, downloaded, or embedded, and saves paper and ink.

READER SURVEY 4

Please visit http://secretreasons.wikispaces.com/Reader+Survey+4 to respond to this survey and encourage teachers in your school or district to respond to the survey, as well.

- Do you use Open Office or some other productivity tools site?
- Do you use Google Docs or some other document-sharing site?
- Do you use Flickr or some other photo-sharing site?
- Has your school embraced the paper-free movement?

If teachers at your school answer predominantly "no" to the above questions, you can have an influence on them by modeling an easy and engaging online tool for them. You can begin to move them forward in Web 2.0 use with an introduction to a simple tool, such as Wordle (http://www.wordle.net/create). See the example beneath this section that I created with a few words describing how easy it is to do! Perhaps you can suggest that teachers paste a list of vocabulary words to the Wordle site, and hit "go" to create a colorful and engaging word cloud that they can project for the class to introduce their next lesson. The simplicity of the process as well as the positive student response may help to motivate them to learn more. Teachers might even find additional lists "in the clouds" on this site that they can use. They can also save their list here "in the clouds" for future access. Your more web-savvy educators can try embedding their word cloud creations on their class websites or blogs, and may even be inspired to create new word cloud lists on a regular basis that students can access from home or school 24/7.

Creighton, 2011

Syndication

Syndication is another significant feature of Web 2.0. Rather than searching for new content related to an area of interest, Internet users can simply subscribe to sites that will then send them updates through RSS feeds. This allows the client a role reversal of receiving updated information rather than constantly searching for it through ever-increasing amounts of data posted online. By subscribing to an RSS feed, users can then customize the amount and type of information they receive regularly. For example, I have created a personal start page through my Google account that is customized so that my Google Reader displays the first line of each new blog post whenever my favorite blogs are updated. My Google Reader searches for new blog posts so that I don't have to do it myself. Using these tools, I can get a quick update each time I log in to Google or Google Chrome. This is the beauty of syndication: it allows items of interest to be directed to you so that you do not have to constantly search for updated information or keep checking your favorite blogs to see if there is a new blog post to read!

How difficult is it to subscribe to an RSS feed? It's easy if you have an email account with Google, Yahoo, AOL, or a similar provider. In Google, for example, simply log in to Google as you would to access your email. At the top of the page, click on "Reader." Locate a blog or website to which you wish to subscribe. In my case, I subscribe to Doug Johnson's "Blue Skunk Blog" and Carl Harvey's "Library Ties," in addition to a number of other blogs. To add blogs like these, I clicked on the "Add a subscription" button on the left-hand side of the page and inserted the URL for these blogs one at a time. My Google Reader then alerts me when a new post has been made to each blog.

Every time I log in to my Google homepage, I have updated blog posts, as well as weather and news updates, the time and temperature outside, and so on. You can do it, too!

READER SURVEY 5

How do you measure up to others in terms of using RSS feeds? Please go to http://secretreasons.wikispaces.com/Reader+Survey+5 to respond to this reader survey.

- Have you established an RSS feed to anything you have posted online?
- Do you subscribe to RSS feeds from others?
- How could using an RSS feed help you in planning for students with special needs, differentiating content, or in customizing lesson plans?

Folksonomy

Tim Berners-Lee (2007) explained that the architecture of the Semantic Web, or Web 2.0, can help to solve the problem of the massive amounts of data that reside on the Internet. Users themselves can help to sort and sift through this data by applying semantic categories, or tags, to the data. Such input helps to connect words, thoughts, and ideas, and to find associations among data sets that make searching for information more productive and less complex. As users tag data, especially with popular search terms and keywords, others can begin to locate more information more easily. This sort of bottoms-up classification is known as "folksonomy" and is the opposite of the top-down taxonomy system of classification that originally dominated the World Wide Web.

Media Sharing

Media sharing is a unique feature of Web 2.0 that allows all types of web-hosted media to be downloaded from or uploaded to social networking sites. It is a process of sharing web-based images, text, apps, games, video, and more. Users simply logon to the Internet through WiFi-ready devices and upload or download their media through the use of text, email, blogs, social networking sites, and more. As media is shared, it often carries tags and comments, which add personal meaning to the media for the benefit of the recipients. An example of media sharing could be as simple as texting a child's photo to another family member with a short note, or as complex as sharing a video game with another video game fan. Media sharing allows users to tag and share content as they are searching the web, or to upload content and immediately alert those in their social networks to its presence on the web. How does this happen? Media sharing can occur because of Web 2.0's unique architecture.

Web 2.0 Architecture

According to Victoria Shannon of the *New York Times*, the Hyptertext Markup Language (HTML) used in the background of each web page is what makes the cross-linking functional. Web page developers had to agree on a precise language used to create sites. Using that common language, sites began to evolve into the interactive social media we see today. Such sites are still evolving, based on traffic and user activity. According to the W3C (www.w3.org/standards/webarch/), HTML (hypertext markup language) and XHTML (extensible hypertext markup language) are the languages that provide the structure of a website, while Cascading Style Sheets (CSS) is the programming that provides the style and layout of the designs. Searching the enormous quantity of data on the Internet is possible through "semantic web technologies" such as Resource Description Framework (RDF), an ontology language for representing data in expressions, SPARQL query language, which is designed to work in conjunction with RDF or OWL (web ontology language), another schema for representing knowledge in a machine-readable format.

However, no technology knowledge is required to understand the way Web 2.0 works and the benefits to users. What is required is acceptance of the participatory nature of Web 2.0 applications and how that concept applies to Internet users, especially in education.

Advertising and Sponsors

Many of the free features of Web 2.0 are paid for by advertising and sponsors. While free gaming and social networking sites are extremely attractive to students, they may also contain advertising aimed at a young audience. Such advertising may pass by Internet filters and may not always be appropriate for educational use. Prior to use, teachers should explore educational sites thoroughly and look for any inappropriate embedded, sidebar, and pop-up advertising. Educators should also be cautioned that advertising may change based on the user's input and anticipate problems in advance. Savvy educators should have a secondary plan in place in the event that a website does feature inappropriate content that escapes institutional filters.

Filtering

The very technology that propelled Google into Web 2.0 mega-stardom also created problems for certain groups of users, such as children. Although the advantages of searching the World Wide Web far outweigh the disadvantages, keeping kids safe online continues to present a challenge for schools. As a result of the Children's Internet Protection Act of 2001, school systems have employed the use of filtering software to allow access to only approved sites on school networks. Filtering sounds like an ideal solution to the safety issue, but it creates its own set of problems. Although they may do a relatively good job of blocking access to dangerous sites, filters can also block access to desirable sites. In addition, filters may not be able to outsmart cunning developers who seek means of naming or coding sites that will pass through filters and still get to their targets.

It may be desirable to keep kids safe online, but teaching students how to discern which sites are safe and which are not is more difficult when the unsafe sites are blocked completely.

The Internet Safety Technical Task Force released a report of online safety in January 2009, which concluded that cyber-bullying and harassment are the worst safety threats faced by youth online. In addition, not all youth are equally endangered. The best predictors of danger online are environment and a child's psychosocial makeup. It would appear that threats to our children's safety are gravely overstated, based on this report. Moreover, if not all children are equally at risk, should all children be equally obstructed from accessing blogs, wikis, social networking sites, and other Web 2.0 tools? According to Collier (2010), today's students are "stereotyped" as "potential victims in a hostile environment," when, in fact, a very few are at risk. For our students to learn good social manners online, they must have the opportunity to practice digital citizenship. The hype about protecting innocents from online predators may actually be fueling a fear of accessing Web 2.0 sites at all. Perhaps our school districts would better serve the next generation by allowing free access and dealing with safety issues when and if they happen.

 READER SURVEY 6

Please go to http://secretreasons.wikispaces.com/Reader+Survey+6 to respond to this survey on filters.

- Do filters prevent access to online content in your district or school?
- How do you teach digital citizenship to your students?

Web 2.0 Teaching Tools to Use Now!

Web 2.0 content includes social networking sites, social bookmarking sites, blogs, wikis, media-sharing sites, document-sharing sites, mashups, folksonomies, virtual worlds, and much more. The concept of online collaboration has spurred the development of new tools that are constantly appearing and morphing as Internet users begin using them. New sites are being added at an astounding rate, with the capacity for interacting with all forms of media, sharing, tagging, and mashing up content as never before.

The following Web 2.0 sites are examples of educator-friendly tools that can be used for instructional purposes. Each has been reviewed for its application in a school setting and its relationship to one or more content standards. While this list is simply a sampling, it is not meant to be a list of the best sites or top recommendations, but rather an assortment to demonstrate the variety and wide application of Web 2.0 in the classroom. Each site is excellent and worth a closer look online.

Animoto

Instead of using desktop application such as Windows Movie Maker, Photostory, or Mac OS's I-movie, educators can inspire their students with the online movie-making site, Animoto. Animoto (http://animoto.

Used with permission from Animoto.com

com/) is an award-winning video presentation tool with multiple special effects, including background music and transitions. The resources provided are easy to use, even for beginners, and make the site ideal for student use. The educational version for use in the classroom is free and allows students to create engaging presentations with professional effects. Animoto can also make instructional content creation easy for teachers and administrators and produces content that is highly engaging to 21st-century students.

Clustrmaps

Instead of using a print map or atlas, educators can engage students with interactive Clustrmaps. Clustrmaps (www.clustrmaps.com/) is a free widget that counts and analyzes the geographic locations of visitors to personal websites or blogs. When embedded on your website or blog, it can be used as a teaching tool to evaluate the extent of cities, countries, and continents you are reaching with your site. Traffic monitoring takes on a 21st-century look and feel with the Clustrmaps widget. Students who post collaborative work online will be interested in the extent of their online audience, as well.

Used with permission from Clustrmaps.com

Used with permission of edublogs.org

Edublogs

Educators can easily engage reluctant writers by having them post their writing assignments on a blog. Edublogs is a free site (www.edublogs.org) that allows users to create and maintain their own blogs. It is highly recommended for students to use, since no email address is needed to set up an account. While other free blogs are open to anyone, edublogs is designed specifically for educational use and includes classroom blog management features and academic functions. In addition, edublogs offers privacy and safety features and is accessible through most district filters.

Flickr Commons

Students needing images for digital storytelling or curriculum-related presentations can find a wealth of them in Flickr Commons. Flickr Commons (www.flickr.com/commons/) is a free resource that contains digitized collections of images from institutions such as Library of Congress, Smithsonian Institution, NASA, NYC Public Library, George Eastman house, and many international institutions. Flickr Commons is an outstanding site for student research and multimedia projects.

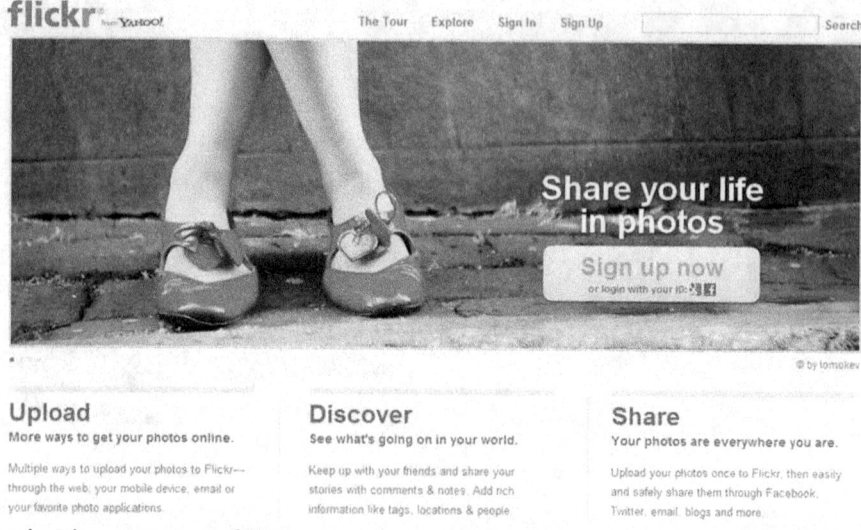

Used with permission of Yahoo.com

Google Docs

Instead of using desktop publishing applications like Microsoft Works or Word, Powerpoint, or Excel, educators can motivate students to collaborate and publish their work for free online by using Google Docs. Google Docs (http://docs.google.com) is a great budget-stretching resource for schools. Internet users simply create a free account and login to the site to create, save, access, and share their documents. Google Docs offers text documents, presentations, spreadsheets,

Used with permission of Google.com

drawings, and embeddable forms for websites and blogs. The sharing feature allows others to collaboratively edit a Google document through an email invitation. Google Docs is cross-platform, converting documents from both Microsoft and Apple formats, as well as Adobe, Autodesk, True Type, XML, and others.

Jason Project

Tired of trying to engage your students in science with a streaming video or DVD? Try the Jason Project instead! The Jason Project (www.jason.org/) is an award-winning science site sponsored by National Geographic and the Sea Research Foundation whose mission is to connect science students with science researchers in a virtual environment. With topics focusing on weather, ecology, energy, and geology, students can experience mission to the sea floor, volcano experiments, and more in real time. Students become so engaged in these events, they scarcely realize they are learning science! The site offers games, videos, lesson plans, and products to buy, and is free, but requires registration.

Used with permission of Jason.org

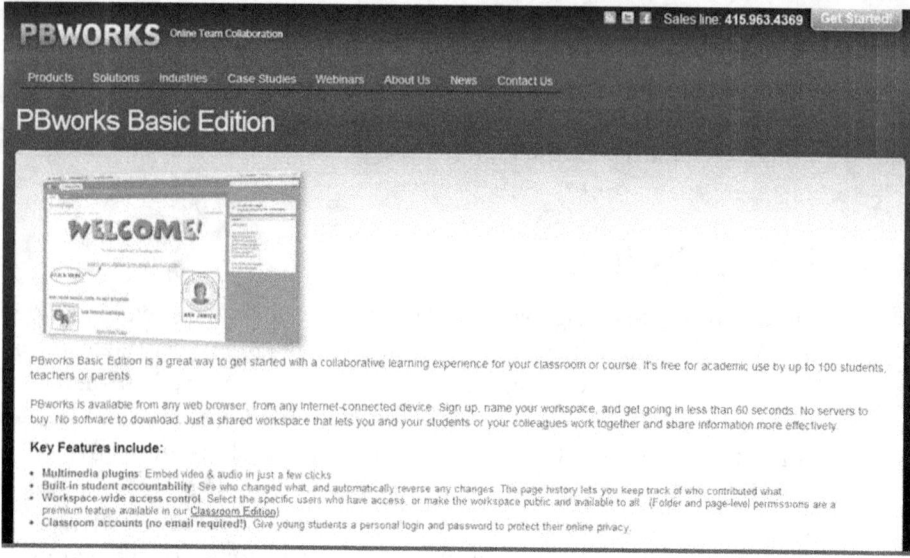

Used with permission of pbworks.com

PBworks

Instead of having students save their work to a folder on their desktop or to a portable flash drive, educators can inspire their students to go a step further and post work to a wiki. PBworks (www.pbworks.com/) is a wiki that is free of advertising and safe for students to use. Using the educational version of PBworks, students can create individual and collaborative web pages, upload videos, images, and text, and post documents. School librarians can post booklists, links, pathfinders, and web quests for staff and student use. School districts can collaboratively share information and resources among schools and across the district and beyond. Free personal wikis offer up to 2G of storage. School and district accounts are by subscription only and vary in cost from $99 to $799 per year.

Prezi

Looking for a great alternative to having students create PowerPoint presentations? Prezi (http://prezi.com) is a free presentation tool that features non-linear presentations created in one continuous workspace. Content is linked with a path tool that allows the presentation to zoom in and out from one item to the next. Text, images, and video can be inserted into presentations. Presentations can be shared with classmates and teachers and presented easily from the web, making Prezi a paperless, or green, option for schools. The site is free for up to 100MB, but offers additional storage and features with a subscription beginning at $59 per year.

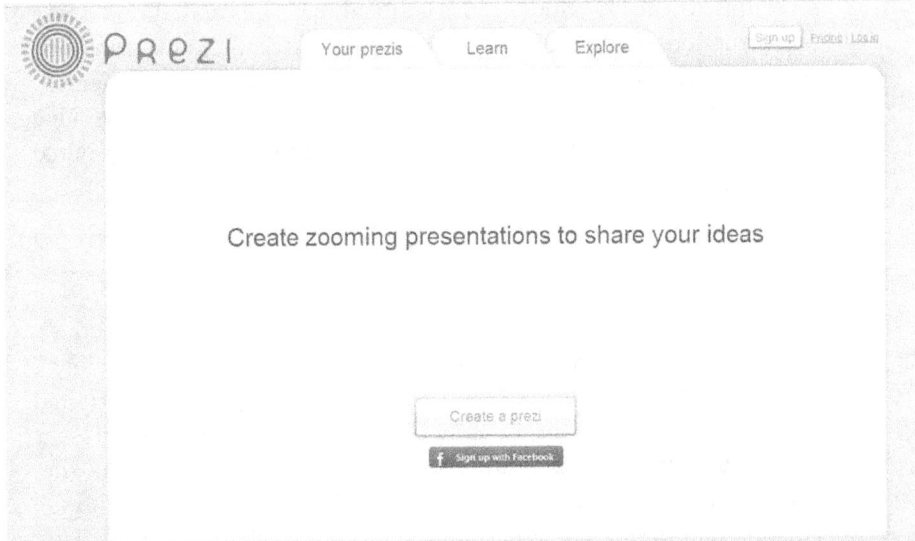

Used with permission of prezi.com

SchoolTube

SchoolTube (www.schooltube.com) is a free video hosting site designed for use by students and teachers in K–12 schools. It offers content

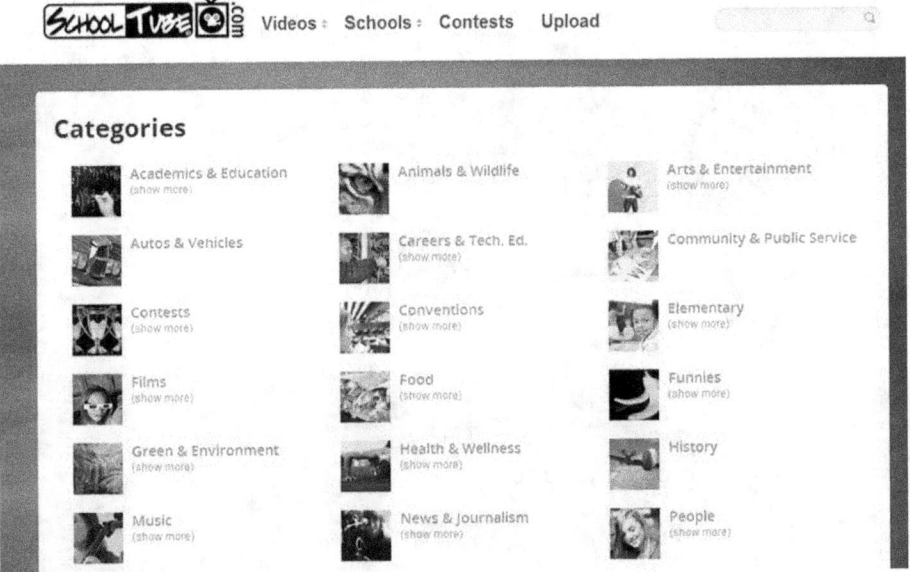

Used with permission of SchoolTube.com

Chapter 1: What Is Web 2.0? 27

screening to ensure safety of instructional materials and allows posting of instructional video such as school news shows, digital storytelling, student research projects, and highlights of school events. Students can search the site for examples and ideas for creating their own video projects. Content is updated regularly and offers a wealth of resources for student projects.

Storybird

Storybird (http://storybird.com/) is a free collaborative storytelling site that allows students to read, write, share, and print their original stories. The site contains a public library of stories that students can read or use for inspirational ideas. Artwork is contained in the site for free use and all files are simply "drag and drop." The site is colorful and highly engaging to 21st-century students. Finished stories can be published online and printed. Storybird includes an optional feature for teachers and parents to monitor and approve their students' work.

Used with permission of Storybird.com

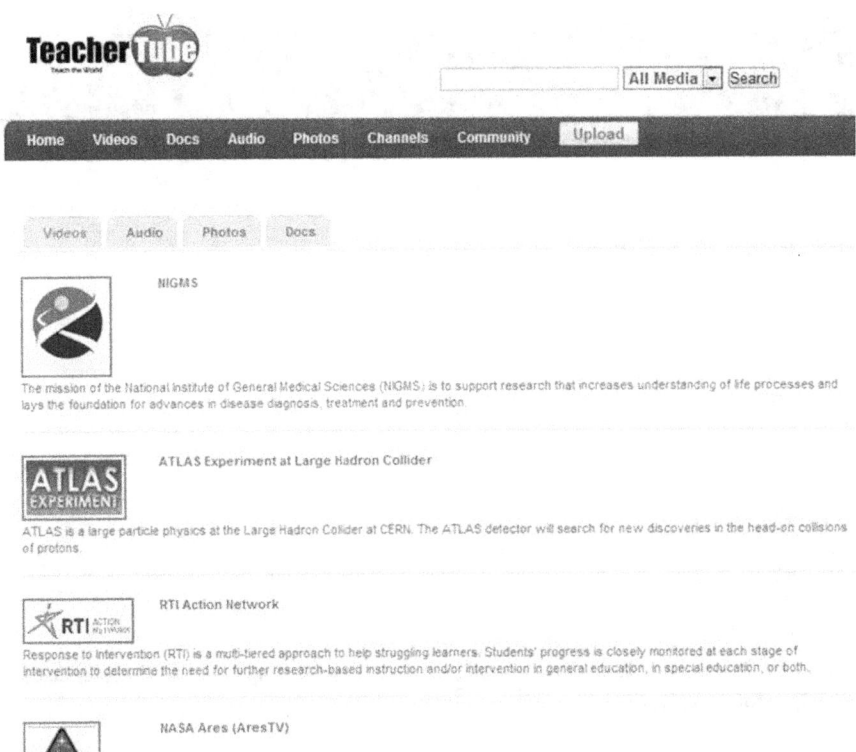

Used with permission of Teachertube.com

TeacherTube

TeacherTube (www.teachertube.com/) is a video hosting and sharing site designed for use by teachers. With channels that identify content by subject and grade level (from elementary through college and professional development) as well as still images, audio, docs, and video, teachers can search for content to enrich their lessons as well as post the exciting and engaging activities they are using in their own classrooms.

Webspiration

Webspiration (www.mywebspiration.com/) is a free (beta version) online visual organizing tool to assist students with writing and research projects. No download is required to create a mindmap or graphic organizer, such as those made with the installable application, Inspiration. Internet users of the Webspiration graphic organizers can share their work and see the work of others. This 21st-century organizer tool is a great way to begin writing and research projects and inspire students to arrange their thoughts and information online "in the clouds."

Used with permission of Inspiration.com

Wordle

Wordle (www.wordle.net/create) is a free word cloud creation site that allows you to select text, fonts, colors, layouts, and the size and shape of the word clouds, edit word clouds in progress, as well as comment

Used with permission of Wordle.net

on word clouds of others. Teacher-created word clouds can be used to highlight blog contents, introduce vocabulary, highlight key words, emphasize passages of text, review important details, introduce main ideas, and more. Finished word clouds can be saved to a public gallery, embedded on a blog or website, or printed out.

Where Do We Go from Here?

An abundance of sites such as the samples above are engaging and content-based as well as free to use, but research indicates that the majority of teachers are not using them. In an article released in June 2010, *eSchool News* (http://learnitin5.com/22-percent-of-teachers-using-technology) reported that only 22 percent of teachers use technology on a regular basis and that 34 percent use it infrequently.

Moreover, school library media specialists, who are often the tech leaders in their schools, are not all using technology tools like these, either. The March/April 2010 issue of *Library Media Connection* (Dickinson, 2010, p. 45) reported the results of its one-question survey: "How Do You Use Social Networking Tools?" with the shocking result that 23.7 percent of school librarians do not use any of these tools at all, 6.3 percent teach about them but do not use them for instruction, and 48.1 percent use them for personal use only. Based on the results of this survey, 78.1 percent of those media specialists surveyed do not use Web 2.0 tools with students.

Such statistics corroborate what Baumbach (2009) found in a survey of Florida media specialists. Of the 631 respondents to her survey, 30 percent never heard of online mapping tools or RSS feeds, and more than 70 percent never taught anyone how to create a blog, wiki, or podcast. Sadly, these statistics reflect a truth about practicing media specialists nationwide: Web 2.0 tools are not commonly used in school libraries.

In the age of connectivism, how can school library media specialists and classroom teachers afford not to use technology for instruction? The reasons for this phenomenon are frustrating and sometimes startling. The reasons teachers are not using technology should be a wake-up call to teacher educators, administrators, school librarians, technology directors, and school boards. It is time to bring classroom instruction into the 21st century! The next chapter will discuss some of the barriers to Web 2.0 use in classroom instruction and highlight recent research on the classroom 2.0 movement. The remaining chapters will introduce the role of the school librarian in modeling, training, and change agentry as schools adapt to 21st-century instructional techniques, including the use of Web 2.0.

Action Steps

The following list outlines possible action steps for school library media specialists, teacher educators, administrators, and others who are interested in motivating more teachers to use Web 2.0 tools for instruction.

- Explore the sites listed in this chapter, considering their application to instruction in your school. Could you initiate a collaborative instructional project with a classroom teacher using at least one of these sites?

- Investigate a feature of Web 2.0 you may not be using, such as an RSS feed. Visit YouTube (www.youtube.com) or Wikihow (www.wikihow.com) to find out how to set up your own RSS feed. Establish a feed for your own blog or subscribe to feeds from the blogs of others using Google Reader or a similar service.

- Try out a different web browser today. If you are not using Firefox, or Google Chrome, for example, explore the possibilities each one offers.

- Try out a different search engine today. Have you explored Bing or Yahoo? Try some searches you have conducted in Google and compare the results with different search engines.

- Take advantage of dynamic code by embedding some widgets on your blog or website. Begin with a calendar, weather, time, or map widget (if you have a Google homepage, try a search of Google gadgets).

- Explore some Web 2.0 applications, such as the ones highlighted earlier in this chapter.

Interactive Features of This Chapter

After you have read this chapter, be sure to visit the online discussion group http://secretreasons.wikispaces.com/message/list/home and post your thoughts about the questions in the "Extending the Conversation" section at the end of the chapter. To join the group, create a free account with wikispaces.com and then add the http://secretreasons.wikispaces.com/ wiki to your account. You can also subscribe to an RSS feed of the page (http://secretreasons.wikispaces.com/) to follow the discussion without joining in.

While the purpose of the group discussion questions are to preview and review the topics in the chapter, they can also be used to stimulate conversation with other professionals. Use this information as a discussion starter in staff meetings and faculty lounges. Link to the wiki to find handouts to share with other professionals and insert the discussion site link above on your blogs and web pages to share this information with others.

Final Thoughts

Never before in history has all of the world's knowledge been so freely available to so many in a form that is immediately accessible and even translatable at the touch of a finger. Digitizing the world's knowledge and then making it socially available has transformed all facets of society, including commerce, health, transportation, national security, and education. This digitized knowledge is readily available worldwide 24/7 through Web 2.0—the collaborative read/write web. Web 2.0 shows great potential to transform education, if integrated into classroom instruction. What remains is to overcome the barriers to Web 2.0 use that confound even the most technologically savvy teachers and administrators. School librarians can play a significant role in overcoming these barriers. To find out more, read on!

Extending the Conversation

Join the online discussion and other activities at http://secretreasons.wikispaces.com/.

Subscribe to the wiki's RSS feed to be notified when new discussion posts appear.

1. What sites do you visit frequently?
2. What sorts of activities do you engage in there?
3. What would you like to see more of online?
4. What would you like to see less of online?
5. Do you use Web 2.0 personally?
6. Do you use Web 2.0 professionally?

7. What barriers have you had to overcome in using Web 2.0?
8. What features of Web 2.0 sites do you like the most?
9. What features of Web 2.0 sites do you like the least?
10. What do you feel would encourage more teachers to teach with Web 2.0?

Teacher Handout: Web 2.0 Teaching Tools to Use Now!

Name of Site	URL	Features
Animoto	http://animoto.com	Award-winning video presentation tool; free, engaging, professional results
Clustrmaps	www.clustrmaps.com/	Widget for tracking geographic locations of web traffic
Edublogs	http://edublogs.org/	Award-winning
Flickr Commons	www.flickr.com/commons/	Large image repository
Google Docs	http://docs.google.com	Great free collaboration tool; replaces need for productivity software
Kid Chatters	www.kidchatters.com	Safe, monitored IM and chat site for students; teach ethical online behavior
Jason Project	www.jason.org	Award-winning; science themed
PBworks	www.pbworks.com	Free and easy wiki for collaborative student projects
Prezi	www.prezi.com	Free, engaging presentation tool
SchoolTube	www.schooltube.com	Free and safe video hosting site; all videos screened; great for student use
Storybird	www.storybird.com	Award-winning; collaborative writing tool
TeacherTube	www.teachertube.com	Free and safe video hosting site; great for teachers
Voki	www.voki.com	Free site for audio recording; digitize directions, vocabulary, more!
Webspiration	www.mywebspiration.com	Graphic organizer by Inspiration
Wordle	www.wordle.net/create	Free word cloud–generator; great for vocabulary lessons

From *The Secret Reasons Why Teachers Are Not Using Web 2.0 Tools and What School Librarians Can Do about It* by Peggy Milam Creighton. Santa Barbara, CA : Libraries Unlimited. Copyright © 2012.

CHAPTER 2

Barriers to Using Web 2.0 in 21st-Century Schools

This chapter will provide an overview of current research on Web 2.0 in schools, particularly focusing on the barriers to Web 2.0 access by classroom teachers and school librarians, as well as the positive impact Web 2.0 has shown on student achievement. Subtopics include:

- Overview of K–12 research
- Barriers to Web 2.0 access in schools
- Current state of technology integration in education

This chapter will focus on answers to the following questions:

- What changes impacted education as a result of Web 2.0?
- Are schools wired for Web 2.0 access?
- Are teachers teaching differently as a result?
- What technologies do teachers use for instruction?
- What technologies do students need to know?

If you are a teacher or a student, you need to know how Web 2.0 affects you now and what changes it will bring in the future. These are great topics to share in a class discussion or in the teacher's lounge! Be sure to join the online discussion and post your thoughts.

The Impact of Web 2.0 on K–12 Education

The changes Web 2.0 brought about in online activities and services extended far beyond state or national communities to affect users around the globe. Access 24/7 has impacted commercial and industrial ventures, transportation, military, medical, and other industries. Once-localized operations have now gone global, with a corresponding effect on the global marketplace. Graduates of 21st-century schools need to be prepared to compete in such a global economy, and schools need the technology tools and teacher training for those tools to effectively prepare them.

The Problem

The Consortium for School Networking (CoSN) organization claims that schools embracing 21st-century technologies can revolutionize learning. In a recent CoSN executive summary, Bosco, Saltpeter, and Mahon-Santos (2010) claim that the lines between the knowledge creators and the knowledge consumers have blurred with the advent of Web 2.0 technologies. But has this revolutionary approach to learning changed teaching and learning in our schools?

According to the National Center for Education Statistics (Rowand, 2000), access to computers has increased and 21st-century classrooms equipped with interactive whiteboards, digital projectors, student response systems, and high-speed Internet access have become increasingly common. In fact, technology-based schools with WiFi networks and full technology integration are rare, but some do exist. The number of such schools is growing.

READER SURVEY 7

Is your school equipped with 21st-century technology such as interactive whiteboards, projectors, and student response systems? Please go to http://secretreasons.wikispaces.com/Reader+Survey+7 to respond to this survey.

High Tech Schools

Tech High in Atlanta, GA (www.techhighschool.org/) is an example of this new breed of schools. A charter school in the Atlanta Public

School system, Tech High formulates the unique curriculum with an emphasis on 21st-century career fields—information technology, communications, and engineering. Its charter status allows Tech High to deviate from the traditional curriculum with waivers to meet the unique needs of its students. Tech High also maintains that success for all is the only course of action for enrolled students. Tech High enrolls approximately 250 students in grades 9–12. While a part of the Atlanta Public School system, Tech High depends on foundations and other organizations for financial support.

The High Technology High School in Lincroft, NJ, is listed as one of *Newsweek*'s best high schools for 2010. Located on the campus of Brookdale Community College through a unique partnership, High Technology High first opened its doors in 1991. It enrolls 240 students in grades 9–12 and has a competitive admissions process for students to enroll in its program. High Technology High is billed as a pre-engineering academy with a curriculum that concentrates on 21st-century fields of science, math, and technology. For more information on High Technology High School, visit www.hths.mcvsd.org/.

The Lowell Milkin High Tech Los Angeles School (www.ht-la.org/index2.jsp) is a Title 1 charter school designed to instruct students in the context of real-world problem-solving. The school's vision is to promote collaboration, technology, communication, and community ethics and responsibility among students. With an enrollment of approximately 350 students, High Tech boasts a 93 percent pass rate on college entrance and advanced placement exams. High Tech Los Angeles is a silver medalist in the *US News and World Report*'s list of best high schools (http://education.usnews.rankingsandreviews.com/best-high-schools/listings/california/high-tech-los-angeles). For more information on the Milkin High Tech LA charter school, visit their website at www.ht-la.org/charter_renewal.jsp.

While the schools above are unusual, every school or school system has had to make adjustments to align with 21st-century student interests. Record amounts have been spent to bring schools into the new millennium. Never before have so many students had access to so many technology resources in schools—interactive whiteboards, ceiling mounted digital projectors, audio and video streaming and recording equipment, digital cameras, document cameras, touch screens, and wireless access have become the norm in most schools. School systems nationwide have invested record amounts of budgets toward becoming 21st-century schools.

At the same time that school systems have increased their number of technology resources and access to technology resources, students have also better access to technology resources through smart phones, portable gaming devices, mini notebook computers, tablet computers, and more. As free wireless is more widely available than ever before, the expectation of accessing the Internet at home or away from home is a greater possibility for many students. Sadly, however, the quality of such access may not have improved at all.

Although access to technology resources in schools has increased, integration of technology resources into instruction has neither increased test scores nor improved instructional quality (Inan & Lowther, 2010). Schools that have embraced technology to individualize instruction are still fewer than the number that have not. According to *eSchool News*, instruction that incorporates Web 2.0 technologies helps students develop 21st-century skills, but the number of schools doing so are still in the minority (Schools Still Conflicted, 2010). Why are schools lagging behind in integrating technology resources into instruction? What is the root cause of this phenomenon and what can be done to bring education to the same level of access as other industries?

Research (Creighton, 2010) cites numerous reasons for this phenomenon, including the excuses most frequently heard from the teachers themselves, such as a lack of time, lack of training, lack of administrative support, and more. Each of these reasons will be addressed individually.

Lack of Time

Busy teachers and school library media specialists have more demands on their time than ever before. Standards-based instruction and differentiation of instruction require significant amounts of time for preparation, resource gathering, and assessment. Accountability policies require tedious recordkeeping and data posting over time from multiple perspectives. It is little wonder that teachers claim they that a lack of time prevents them from using Web 2.0 (Brinkerhoff, 2006; Brodie, 2006)? What are the conditions like in your situation?

READER SURVEY 8

Please go to http://secretreasons.wikispaces.com/Reader+Survey+8 to respond to this survey.

- Do you have a planning period during the school day?
- Do you have a duty-free lunch period?

- Are you required to attend after school meetings?
- Does your school or district provide curriculum planning days for you?
- Are you required to attend evening events, such as PTA meetings?
- What other constraints on your time do you face as a teacher?

Lack of Training

Budget cuts and personnel cuts may mean that technology funding and technology support personnel no longer exist in many areas. Busy teachers have little time to wait for someone to make repairs or advise them when technology fails. Given such a lack of support, many teachers opt for the tried-and-true and revert to instruction that omits technology altogether (Creighton, 2010), or simply include it in a center or workstation for students to visit. As greater budget cuts are made in the future and existing technology support personnel retire and are not replaced, technology training and support may become a thing of the past. Is it any wonder that teachers claim they do not have the skills or support they need to integrate technology into instruction?

READER SURVEY 9

Please go to http://secretreasons.wikispaces.com/Readers+Survey+9 to respond to this survey.

- Does your school or district provide technology training for teachers?
- If so, is it free?
- If so, is it available during the school day?
- If so, is it offered online or face to face?
- If not, how and where do teachers obtain the technology training they need?

TIP

A significant amount of technology training is now freely available on the web for teachers to access 24/7. Sites such as YouTube and TeacherTube contain videos with step-by-step directions that can be viewed while at your computer for hands-on, real-time training. A great site for award-winning technology training is www.freetech4teachers.com/.

Lack of Technology Support

As teachers begin to experiment more with technology and use it on a regular basis, some items are bound to break down. At the same time, with budget cuts threatening to stretch school budgets to the limit, technology support may be reduced or nonexistent. In such cases, what happens when technology fails to work? All too often, the problems are relatively simply to fix, but teachers may not have the time, skills, or administrative rights to fix the problem (Creighton, 2010). The result is that when technology fails, technology integration fails, as well.

READER SURVEY 10

Please go to http://secretreasons.wikispaces.com/Reader+Survey+10 to respond to this survey.

- Do you have technology support personnel in your school or district?
- If not, how do you solve technology problems?
- If so, how many teachers are served by each tech support person?

TIP

Tech support can be accomplished even with a low budget or no budget. Numerous blogs and websites offer free advice for solving technology problems, and students can often be trained to serve as tech support personnel, as well. Be sure to document the steps taken to resolve a problem, including a detailed description of the problem, for future use as a problem-solving manual.

Lack of Administrative Support

Similar to a lack of technology support is a lack of administrative support. If a school administrator focuses primarily on student achievement, technology integration may or may not be a part of that focus (Lockerby, Lynch, Sherman, & Nelson, 2004; Todd, 2008; Buzzeo, 2008), particularly if the administrator is not technology-savvy. Without an administrator emphasizing its use, technology integration into instruction may be put on the back burner or used only on special occasions, rather than on a daily basis, and both teachers and students will suffer for it.

> **TIP**
>
> Use the following handout, "Research on Administrator Support for Technology Integration," to demonstrate your principal's influence on technology use in instruction. Share the handout with each administrator and with all staff members. Post the handout to your blog and keep extra copies in a prominent place, such as the mailroom or teacher's lounge.

RESEARCH ON ADMINISTRATOR SUPPORT FOR TECHNOLOGY INTEGRATION

Factor	Research citations
School culture	http://outreach.msu.edu/bpbriefs/issues/brief31.pdf
	http://wmpeople.wm.edu/asset/index/mxtsch/beckersmith
Tech training	http://www.iel.org/programs/21st/reports/principal.pdf
Scheduling	http://www.educationworld.com/a_admin/admin/admin528.shtml
Facilitation	http://www.cited.org/index.aspx?page_id=187
Apprenticeship	http://www.cited.org/index.aspx?page_id=185
Classroom observations	http://www.educationworld.com/a_admin/columnists/young/young005.shtml
Goal-setting	http://www.wallacefoundation.org/Pages/1_3-patterns-of-distributed-leadership-learning-from-leadership.aspx
Budgeting	http://paws.wcu.edu/churley/budgets.html
Policies and Procedures	http://www.edweb.net/fimages/op/PrincipalsandSocialNetworkingReport.pdf
	http://www.wallacefoundation.org/Pages/1_3-patterns-of-distributed-leadership-learning-from-leadership.aspx
	http://www.scholastic.com/teachers/article/role-principal
Modeling	http://www.scholastic.com/teachers/article/role-principal
	http://www.educationworld.com/a_admin/admin/admin466_a.shtml
Incentives	http://www.educationworld.com/a_admin/admin/admin268.shtml

READER SURVEY 11

Please go to http://secretreasons.wikispaces.com/Reader+Survey+11 to respond to this survey.

- Does your administration support technology innovations, such as Web 2.0 use?
- How strict is your administrator about technology integration into instruction?
- Does your school have a technology plan?
- Are you on your school's technology committee?
- Does your school or district sponsor a technology fair?
- Do you have interactive whiteboards and projectors?
- Do teachers have laptops for instructional use?
- Do students have laptops for instructional use?
- Is your school equipped with WiFi?

TIP

A great resource for tips on developing a positive relationship with your principal is: www.nea.org/tools/38737.htm.

School Culture

School culture may dictate where and when technology is integrated into instruction (Anderson, 2007; Lockerby et al., 2004). The PTA may be the main provider of funding for technology and the most popular teachers are the ones earmarked for receipts from PTA for technology spending. Or, the upper grades in the school might be the ones whose classrooms are equipped with technology, while the primary grades share a limited number of computers in centers. One school may have a computer lab that is always filled up before all teachers can get a chance to take a class. Another may have three computers per classroom and very large classes, making it difficult for all students to access them regularly. Upper schools might have separate buildings, with the computer labs not easily accessible for those the farthest from them. Certain high schools may focus on the arts, science, and math, or have a literacy focus rather than a technology focus. Even the most tech-savvy teacher cannot buck the school culture for long.

READER SURVEY 12

Please go to http://secretreasons.wikispaces.com/Reader+Survey+12 to respond to this survey.

- Is your school a technology-focused school?
- Is your school a literacy-focused school?
- Is your school a magnet school for science and/or math?
- Is your school a magnet school for the arts?
- Do parents volunteer in your school?
- What is the focus of your school's culture?
- Is your school open and collaborative or divided up into departments, grade levels, or teams?

TIP

School culture can be daunting and pervasive. Be a joiner rather than a fighter. Joining in with groups and events allows you to be seen as a member of the group and builds trust. It can also open doors for you that might otherwise be closed. A great resource for developing understanding of school culture is www.smallschoolsproject.org/PDFS/culture.pdf.

While a number of issues may help to explain the lack of improvement from technology integration, one of the most pervasive is commonly known as the digital divide.

The Digital Divide

In spite of massive expenditures on technology resources, the digital divide still exists in schools. Not all schools are comparably equipped. Students who may rely on access through a public source such as a community center or public library will find that not all public libraries or community centers are comparably equipped, just as not all homes are comparably equipped. Perhaps none of these sites will ever be comparably equipped, but the ones who suffer the most from inequalities such as this are those with limited resources and little or no access from home. At the same time, some individuals who cannot access technology resources from home or a public library may have access through other internet-ready resources such as a PDA (personal digital assistant; handheld computer), Smartphone, or other portable computing device. Such access allows them to stay abreast of new technologies as they appear and to develop skills with them while those without access do not. As those with access become more adept with navigating and using new tools, the gap between the haves and have-nots widens. This is the essence of the digital divide.

Fortunately, more and more personal computing devices are wired for Internet access. Smartphones, iPads, Kindles, PSPs (Playstation Portable), and more are now wired for mobile Internet access. At the same time, an increasing number of public gathering spots and retail centers are attracting customers with free wireless access. According to a recent report from the Pew Research Center, mobile Internet access is increasing, particularly among African Americans and Latinos. Taking photos and sending text messages are the most popular mobile activities, but accessing the Internet came in third.

For more information on the Pew Research or to read the full Pew Research Center report, visit www.pewinternet.org/Reports/2010/Mobile-Access-2010.aspx.

TIP

Smartphones can help bridge the digital divide. Smartphones are convenient teaching tools, offering calculators, eBook readers, podcasting, vodcasting, and online resource access. Smartphones can even be turned into inexpensive student response systems! For more information, see www.edweek.org/dd/articles/2011/02/09/02apps.h04.html.

READER SURVEY 13

Please go to http://secretreasons.wikispaces.com/Reader+Survey+13 to respond to this survey.

- What barriers do you face in Web 2.0 access at your school?
- Do you students have access to the Internet at home?
- Are your students allowed to bring cell phones to school?

- Does your school have WiFi (wireless Internet access)?
- Is your school using tools such as eBook readers, Digital audio players, and gaming systems?
- Does your school have a low-income population?
- What steps, if any, are being taken in your district to address the digital divide?

Although the digital divide may be closing, it is still wide open in many areas of this country. Families living in poverty rarely have access to a computer and the Internet. With the recent downturn in this nation's economy, the number of families living in poverty has reached an all-time high of 14.3 percent, according to the U.S. Census Bureau (www.census.gov/hhes/www/poverty/poverty.html). Children living in poverty make up the largest percentage of those living in poverty: more than 11 percent in all states, and higher in the states of Alabama, New Mexico, Kentucky, Arkansas, and Mississippi. In fact, only 9 percent of all homes in Mississippi have broadband Internet access, compared to a national average of 20 percent. An online report by the Children's Partnership website breaks down the severity of the problem in a state-by-state snapshot: www.childrenspartnership.org/Content/Navigation Menu/Programs/Technology/State_Fact_Sheets.htm.

Will increasing the level of Internet access help resolve this issue? Probably not, according to Wright (2010). The quality of access is also important. If online activity is used only for downloading video, as opposed to gaining information, than the increased access does little to lessen the digital divide.

Digital Divide in Schools

According to a report in PBS's *Frontline*, the secretary of education claimed that the digital divide consists of a lack of opportunity in school, after school, as well as at home. The way to end the cycle of poverty is to make our schools a place to provide the opportunity these students lack. See the entire report at www.pbs.org/wgbh/pages/front line/digitalnation/learning/schools/the-new-digital-divide.html?play

The digital divide will not end simply with providing opportunities unless there is a training component, as well. Although some states have made strides in providing computers and access to the Internet, there remains a gap in how technology is being used in schools. State

Table 2.1: Reasons for Not Integrating Technology in Education

Teachers Claim	Other Factors
Lack of time	School culture
Lack of training	Digital divide
Lack of technology support	Unequal funding
Lack of administrative support	Varying backgrounds
District policies and filters	Network issues
Fear of unknown	Age and experience of faculty

and federal programs have increased the number and quality of educational technology resources, but those resources are not being used equitably. In poorer school districts, according to *Education Week* (Trotter, 2007), the most common use of technology resources is for repetitive drill exercises such as math multiplication table practice In more affluent schools, the technology resources are used more for problem-solving exercises. Today's students, however, need more than repetitive practice or problem-solving online. They need access to and practice with real-world applications such as they will be using after graduation. Twenty-first-century schools must prepare students for the new and emerging workforce. Upon graduation, students must be able to compete globally with candidates who might be willing to work for less, to commute farther, or to extend their education in order to become more skilled.

At the same time, teachers are being challenged to learn new technologies and integrate them into instruction to keep students motivated and engaged in learning. Some districts are funding training for teachers to glean new skills with technology, but many more are not addressing training at all. Budget cuts in many areas have forced districts to slash funding for instructional technology departments and have offered little support in place of the technology trainers that were dismissed from payrolls. As a result, teachers frequently offer excuses for not integrating technology into instruction (see Table 2.1).

The Solution and Potential Applications

A recent report from the National Coordination Office for Networking and Information Technology Research and Development (NITRD) made recommendations for resolving the digital divide, including suggestions such as using constructivist approaches to classroom instruction. A constructivist approach involves students constructing knowledge collaboratively with other students. In a constructivist learning environment, group work and project-based learning is the norm, rather than students working independently. See the entire report at www.nitrd.gov/pubs/pitac/digital_divide/pres-2 feb00-ddlrecs.html.

Web 2.0 resources are well suited for this collaborative, constructivist approach to learning. Students could work in groups and jointly create a wiki of their learning on a topic. They could post to a blog and respond to each other's posts, exchanging thoughts and ideas. They could read and comment on each other's writing, collaboratively assessing their work on a common rubric. They could work in pairs to solve math word problems and post their work to a course management site where all could see the different approaches to solving the problem and discuss their thoughts on each. Numerous free Web 2.0 tools allow for all of these approaches to learning, and many more. The advantages of using Web 2.0 in education are extensive.

Advantages of Web 2.0

Web 2.0 tools can be a part of an individualized program that addresses unique student needs. Blind students or students who need reading support strategies can enable a read-aloud toolbar, for example.

Web 2.0 tools support a constructivist learning environment that allows students to create their own knowledge from a wealth of resources. For example, Web 2.0 tools provide access to resources outside of the classroom such as authors, scientists, museums, and laboratories all over the world.

Web 2.0 tools provide an authentic audience for student work, drawing readers from all over the globe who can comment on and edit student work. Students can receive objective commentary and can compare their work to that of others to help improve the quality of work they produce.

Web 2.0 tools present an opportunity for students to collaborate with others in a real-world environment. Such collaboration will be a part of the 21st-century workplace, so familiarity with Web 2.0 and collaborative work will better prepare students for future employment.

> **TIP**
>
> For more on the advantages of using Web 2.0 in education, visit http://web2darkside.wetpaint.com/page/Advantages+of+Web+2.0+Tools and www.slideshare.net/sachac/a-teachers-guide-to-web-20-at-school.

21st-Century Skills

The Partnership for 21st Century Skills (2009) developed the *Framework for 21st Century Learning*, which identified such skills as the following required for graduates entering the workforce:

- Creativity and innovation
- Critical thinking and problem solving
- Communication and collaboration
- Information, Communication, Technology, and Media literacy
- Flexibility and adaptability
- Initiative and self-direction
- Social and cross-cultural skills
- Productivity and accountability
- Leadership and responsibility

By using Web 2.0 tools on a regular basis, students will be able to develop skills in cooperating and collaborating with others, in solving problems and utilizing critical thinking skills, in becoming more self-directed, creative, productive, and responsible, and in developing media literacy, information literacy, and technology literacy skills at the same time. Is it not ironic that the very skills students will need to develop are being hindered by a lack of access to technology and Web 2.0 tools that would enable them to develop? The most compelling reasons for integrating Web 2.0 into instruction is that it affords students the opportunity to develop 21st-century skills—the very skills they will need to be competitive in the workforce.

For more information on the Partnership for 21st Century Skills, visit their website: www.p21.org/.

National Educational Technology Standards

The International Society for Technology in Education has developed the National Educational Technology Standards (NETS) for students, teachers, and administrators. Similar to the Partnership for 21st Century Skills' dispositions, the ISTE NETS focuses on the skills our students will need to compete in a global marketplace. The complete list of standards can be found at www.iste.org/standards.aspx.

The American Association of School Librarians (AASL) has developed its Standards for 21st-Century Learners, with a similar focus on the skills and dispositions of 21st-century learners, available at: www.ala.org/ala/mgrps/divs/aasl/guidelinesandstandards/learningstandards/standards.cfm.

However, the potential of Web 2.0 tools to alleviate the digital divide in education may be unrealized because of the barriers school systems face when seeking to provide Web 2.0 access safely to their students. Concerns that elevate safety above access may explain why 21st-century schools are still in the minority.

Disadvantages of Web 2.0

While Web 2.0 tools have created some profitable collaborative benefits to use, they also have a downside. Popular Web 2.0 tools have created some interesting negative phenomena: viral postings (that crash sites with traffic), social network addiction, spam, and cyber-bullying, to name a few. Part of the problem is related to the social nature of Web 2.0. When anyone anywhere has the ability to post and edit a site, some problems are inevitable. Moreover, widespread participation can be inappropriate for all audiences, making it difficult for schools to join in freely. As a response, a number of .edu sites have appeared, with versions of popular applications aimed at educational use only. However, spam and cyber-bullying has even made its way into educational sites, and school filters cannot catch all inappropriate postings.

Other problems have cropped up with Web 2.0 use in schools. As more and more students become involved with access to Web 2.0 on school networks, problems such as copyright infringement, cyber theft, and identity theft have become increasingly common. Educators must teach student users to behave appropriately online and to protect themselves even in educational sites. Filters cannot always keep students safe. Educators and parents must warn students that free sites are not completely free. The advertising that makes a site available to them without cost may also attempt to sell them goods or save information about their web-based activities. Educators and parents must also warn students that copyright infringements can happen anywhere, as can cyber theft, and instruct students on copyright law and the potential for cyber theft and identity theft online. Even young students should be cautioned about Internet safety and digital citizenship (see Table 2.2).

Table 2.2: Advantages and Disadvantages of Web 2.0 in Education

Advantages	**Disadvantages**
Collaborative	Viral postings (that crash sites with traffic)
Real-world experience	Social network addiction
Individualized	Spam
Constructivist	Cyber-bullying
Worldwide resource-based	Copyright infringements
Authentic audience	Cyber theft
Engaging	Inappropriate advertising
Social vetting	Limited security
Cost reduction	Limited content control
Ubiquitous	Variations in quality of content
Expands resources available	Lack of content governance
Prepares students for 21st-century workforce	Dependable high speed WiFi access required

From *The Secret Reasons Why Teachers Are Not Using Web 2.0 Tools and What School Librarians Can Do about It* by Peggy Milam Creighton. Santa Barbara, CA : Libraries Unlimited. Copyright © 2012.

For more details on the disadvantages of Web 2.0 use in schools, visit: www.exforsys.com/tutorials/web-2.0/advantages-and-disadvantages-of-web-2.0.html and www.wired.com/science/discoveries/news/2005/10/69366.

Although the criticisms and challenges are many in adopting Web 2.0 into classroom instruction, the benefits outweigh them simply because students who develop expertise with Web 2.0 tools will be prepared to enter the 21st-century workforce. If our schools and school districts continue to inhibit widespread access, teacher training, and full technology integration, our students will not be able to compete with graduates from other countries. Jobs will go to those who whose skills match the demands of the workforce—those who can conduct business online, seek information effectively, create products, and collaborate with others around the world. The future of our children is at stake! We can no longer afford to wait for change to happen. The world is changing around us and the state of education must change with it or our students will be left behind, with or without lawmakers enforcing more assessments.

The next chapter will discuss School Library 2.0 theory and the role of the web-savvy school librarian in effecting a positive social change by in adopting Web 2.0 into 21st-century instruction.

Action Steps

- Examine the technology plan for your school or district. Where do the AASL and ISTE NETS standards converge with your school or district standards? Where do they differ?
- What can be done to see that access is unblocked to specific sites in your district?
- Meet with your library committee to forge a document that embeds the AASL and ISTE standards as they converge with district standards.
- Discuss the committee document with your principal.
- Prioritize goals for your students to develop 21st-century information literacy and technology skills.

Extending the Conversation

Join the online discussion at http://secretreasons.wikispaces.com/.
Subscribe to the wiki's RSS feed to be notified when new discussion posts appear.

1. Do you feel the digital divide can be resolved? Why or why not?
2. What skill sets do you feel 21st-century students must acquire prior to graduation?
3. What impact has the global economy had on your personal use of the Internet?
4. What technology training do you still need to effectively integrate technology in your current position?
5. Is you school or district equipped with 21st-century technology? Explain.
6. What advantages of Web 2.0 do you see for use in schools?
7. What disadvantages do you see?
8. Have you experienced problems with cyber-bullying or other inappropriate Internet use with students?

CHAPTER 3

School Library 2.0

This chapter will discuss School Library 2.0 theory, detail its implications for 21st-century school librarians, and provide examples of its use in school libraries, with screenshots and links to resources. Subtopics include:

- School Library 2.0 theory
- Implications for 21st-century school librarians
- Samples of Web 2.0 tools for school libraries
- Screenshots and links

School librarians are frequently the technology leaders in their schools, and are often the first to adopt new technologies into their practice. The advent of Web 2.0 has brought about numerous tools that appeal to school libraries. Taking library services into the clouds (or online), using blogs, wikis, IM, texting, social bookmarking, and social networking to connect with patrons is known as School Library 2.0.

- Is your school library program as relevant as it once was?
- Have you moved your library program into the 21st century?
- Do you incorporate the latest technologies into instruction and services?

These strategies form the basis of the School Library 2.0 movement. If you are not sure whether your program is incorporating everything it can to be relevant to today's patrons, or even how Web 2.0 fits into your library program, this chapter has been written for you! Be sure to join the online discussion and post your response to the questions at the end of this chapter.

Web 2.0

O'Reilly and Dougherty (O'Reilly, 2005) introduced the idea of Web 2.0 in 2004 at a conference brainstorming session, but the term soon became a descriptor for a user-focused web where dynamic new technologies are used to communicate and collaborate with content online. As explained in chapter 1, dynamic technologies result in web content that changes based on user input. For example, as a Google user types in a search term, dynamic programming searches for related sidebar ads that pop up to attract the user. Similarly, Amazon users find "You might also like" suggestions for purchases, and MapQuest users find restaurant and entertainment suggestions in the area of the address they seek. Such content then becomes more personal and pertinent to users, as well as more likely to return items of interest in searches. One of the most popular features of Web 2.0 is social networking.

Social Networking Theory

Social networking is the act of joining a community of users in order to interact with other users by sharing information, media, news, and other items. Social networking theory proposes that individuals join other like-minded individuals to interact, building a web of contacts. The extent of an individual's contacts can determine the value, or social capital, of those contacts. According to Maness (2006), the theory of social networking suggests that there are many different kinds of social relationships within a social network and some of the individuals in those relationships have greater influence than do others. The theory of social networking also suggests the greater the number of Internet users a site has, the greater the value of the site to its members (Maness, 2006). Moreover, the visitors to a social networking site create additional value by bringing in their own social contacts and, thus, enlarging the network.

Social networking can help to make school library sites more engaging and collaborative for patrons. By shifting catalogs and online resources to a social networking format, school libraries can create an online presence where users can access resources, post comments, collaborate with other patrons, tag resources with keywords, and upload new contents in a virtual library community (Aharony, 2008; Farkas, 2007; Naslund & Giustini, 2008).

School Library 2.0

School librarians can practice School Library 2.0 theory by establishing an online school library community using IM and chat, commenting and tagging, streaming media and sharing media, and other social networking features. The interactive online features will engage 21st-century school library patrons and enable them to access library resources 24/7 from any location. The collaborative and interactive online environment is what distinguishes a school library 2.0 from an ordinary library website (Naslund & Giustini, 2008).

Even though some innovative school libraries have gone online with their services, the majority of school libraries have not. School Library 2.0 theory implies that engaging 21st-century learners and meeting their needs should be reason enough to transfer any program to the web, incorporating streaming media, file-sharing, dynamic web-based resources, chat and IM reference services, dynamic web-based resources, screen-cast tutorials, social media, and other user-centric, real-time services (Farkas, 2007; Hastings, 2008; Maness, 2006). However, district technology policies and filters have restricted many school librarians from making such a move. In their review of school libraries providing online services, *American Libraries* claimed that state legislatures often forbid schools to provide students access to social networking and chat rooms if they receive e-rate funding (House Passes Bill, 2006). Such policies and filters represent one barrier school libraries face in providing 21st-century services, although there are many other barriers that school librarians typically struggle to overcome. These barriers and some potential solutions to them will be discussed more fully in chapter 4.

Implications for School Librarians

School librarians can no longer ignore the direction of the read-write web, even if district filters prohibit access at school. In response to the needs of interests of 21st-century students, school librarians can increase the relevance of their libraries by integrating the use of Web 2.0 tools into their practice and embedding widgets or links to them on their school library home pages. The following tools are of particular interest to school librarians at all levels and are engaging to readers everywhere. These tools can be a starting point for adopting School Library 2.0 into your own programs.

Web 2.0 Tools for School Librarians and Readers to Use Now!

The Book Seer

The Book Seer (http://bookseer.com/) is a free interactive site that links books with readers by suggesting similar titles or genres when a title is entered. The site uses recommendations from Amazon and LibraryThing and refers users to their local library or bookstore for a personal recommendation. This site is a great resource for readers' advisory 24/7 and provides a starting point for face-to-face readers' advisory conversations. Students will enjoy using this site to find another title similar to ones they have enjoyed.

Used with permission of bookseer.com

Used with permission of booktalk.org

BookTalk

BookTalk (www.booktalk.org/) is a free site where readers can talk online about their favorite books in a collaborative group discussion. The site features live author chats, links to publishers, book blogs, audiobooks, eBooks, booksellers, games, and more. Follow BookTalk on Facebook and Twitter.

Bookwink

Bookwink (http://bookwink.com/) is a book trailer site that promotes books and reading by previewing each title with a bit of author and content information in a podcast or vodcast format, complete with background music and sound effects. This free site is arranged by subject or grade level, is an award-winner, and will definitely spark students' interests in a variety of genres. Great for librarians to use in collection development, too!

Used with permission of bookwink.com

Used with permission of digital booktalk.com

Digital BookTalk

Digital BookTalk (www.digitalbooktalk.com) is a book trailer site that offers video reviews of approximately 100 books for middle school and young adult readers. A few titles may be appropriate for upper elementary readers. Most of the videos were produced by adults, but the site indicates approximately 20 videos were created by students. Digital BookTalk currently has over 2,500 members and now offers training for teachers and media specialists on how to create their own digital book trailers.

Goodreads

Goodreads (www.goodreads.com) is a free site that allows members to create their own bookshelves of books they are reading, want to read, or have read, as well as browse similar shelves of others. Members can post book reviews, participate in a discussion group, interact with an author or write and post their own work for others to review. Goodreads solicits the work of librarians to enhance their cataloging data and provides a librarian manual on site. Goodreads also posts literary quotes, trivia quizzes, literary events, bookswaps, and more. With its listopia feature, members can vote for their favorite titles and create genre lists.

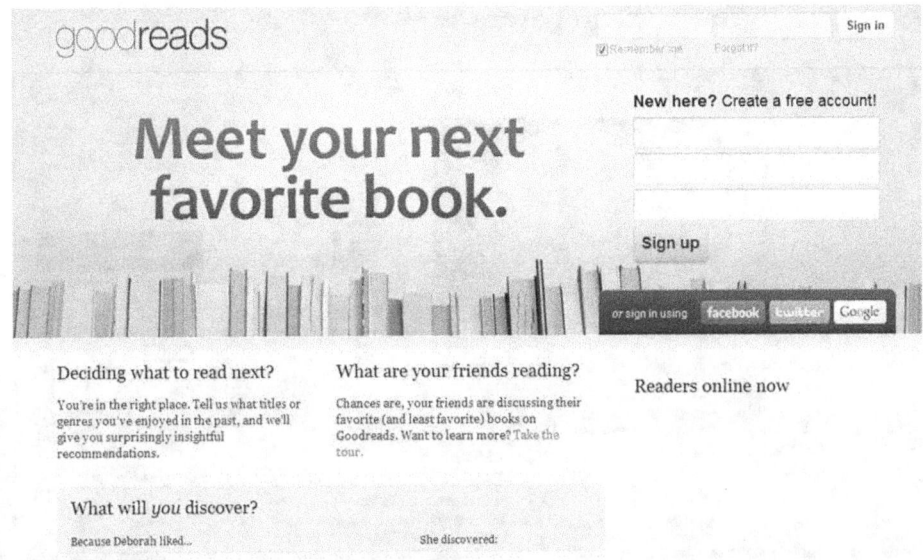

Used with permission of Goodreads.com

Google Books

Google Books (http://books.google.com) is a free service that offers millions of digitized books and magazines, many of which are full-text. The free access version provides a preview of millions of books, while the full-text versions are available for a fee.

Used with permission of Google.com

Used with permission of Google LitTrips.com

Google LitTrips

Google LitTrips (www.googlelittrips.org/) is a bookmapping site that locates the events in literature on Google Earth—a 3D digital world map based on satellite images. The lit trip incorporates annotations on book characters and events through placemarkers or multimedia links with descriptive information that help readers to immerse themselves into the geographical, historical, and personal context of a story.

The International Children's Digital Library

The International Children's Digital Library (http://en.childrenslibrary.org/) is a free site that features digital children's books in a multitude of languages. The goal of the site is to build tolerance for all nations and cultures by featuring high-quality digital children's books in every language. The current collection includes more than 4,000 books in 55 languages, with patrons from more than 200 countries. Users can search for books by country, keyword, awards, authors and illustrators, collections, and more.

Used with permission of the International Children's Digital Library.org

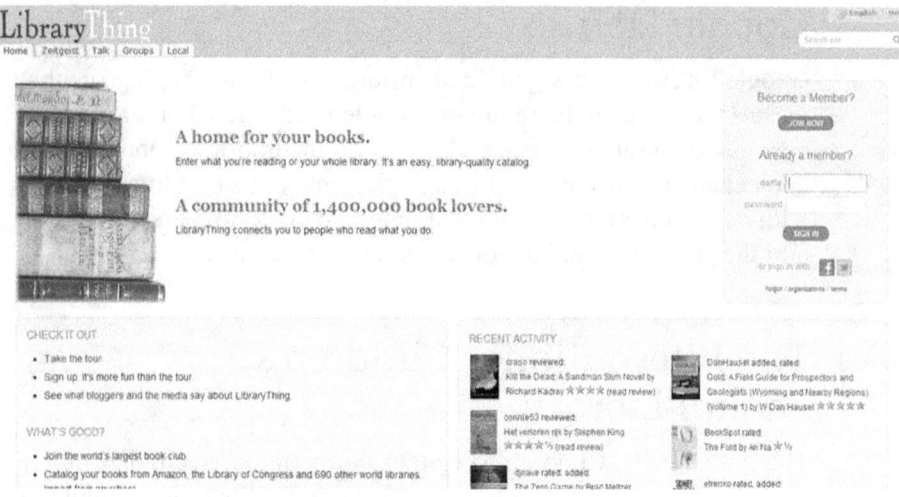
Used with permission of LibraryThing.com

LibraryThing

LibraryThing (www.librarything.com) is a free cataloging site that features a collaborative community of more than 1 million book lovers. Members can catalog their home library collection, their favorite books, their summer reading lists, their school library collection (over 200 books requires a fee), or whatever list of titles they may choose. Features of the site include book reviews, cover images, author interactivity, discussion boards, groups, ratings, and more. LibraryThing is popular for its book reviews and groups as well as the ability to catalog your collection using recognized systems such as the Library of Congress or the Dewey Decimal System. LibraryThing offers a mobile app and a personal bookshelf widget you can post to your blog. Follow LibraryThing on Facebook.

The Online Books Page: Book Listings

The Online Books Page (http://onlinebooks.library.upenn.edu/) offers more than 1 million free digitized books. While not specifically designed for children, this collection does maintain a children's books section, including some periodicals such as *Bulletin of the Center for Children's Books*, poetry, plays, and short stories.

The Online Books Page
onlinebooks.library.upenn.edu

Listing over 1 million free books on the Web - Updated Friday, November 11, 2011

BOOKS ONLINE
Search our Listings -- New Listings -- Authors -- Titles -- Subjects -- Serials

NEWS
We reach one million listings -- Blog (Everybody's Libraries) -- Latest Book Listings

FEATURES
A Celebration of Women Writers -- Banned Books Online -- Prize Winners Online

ARCHIVES AND INDEXES
General -- Foreign Language -- Specialty

THE INSIDE STORY
About Us -- FAQ -- Get Involved! -- Suggest a Book -- In Progress/Requested -- More Links

Edited by John Mark Ockerbloom (onlinebooks@pobox.upenn.edu)
OBP copyrights and licenses

Used with permission of the OnlineBookspage

Podiobooks

Podiobooks (www.podiobooks.com/) features audio podcasts of complete books in segments, or episodes designed for RSS feeds. The feeds can be burned to a CD for use on a computer workstation or downloaded to an MP3 player for individual or small group use in a listening center. The site features books for adults and children in a variety of genres. Podiobooks is free, but donations are solicited to offset the costs of publishing and to provide payments to authors. Librarians will find this a good source for previewing books and for teaching staff and students about podcasts.

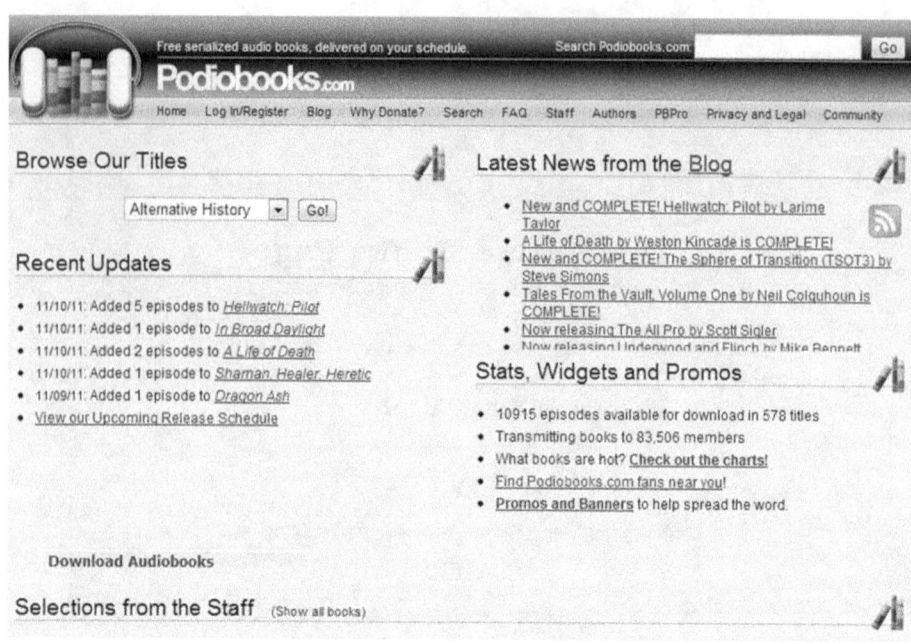

Used with permission of podiobooks.com

Used with permission of Reading Rockets.org

66 *The Secret Reasons Why Teachers Are Not Using Web 2.0 Tools*

Reading Rockets

Reading Rockets (www.readingrockets.org/) is a free, government-sponsored site that provides a wealth of reading resources for parents, teachers, administrators, librarians, and others interested in children's reading development. The site features videos and podcasts, books and authors, research, reading guides, daily quizzes, and more. The site also has a Facebook fan page.

Scholastic Book Wizard

Scholastic Book Wizard (http://bookwizard.scholastic.com/tbw/home Page.do) makes it easy to level books for students. The site features a quick search tool that allows searching by author, title, or keyword, as well as a Bookalike tool that locates similar titles on the same reading level. The site also allows teachers to create booklists, share lists, and level their classroom libraries. Book Wizard now features a widget (www.scholastic.com/tbwwidget/) that can be embedded on school or classroom blogs.

Used with permission from Scholastic.com. 2011

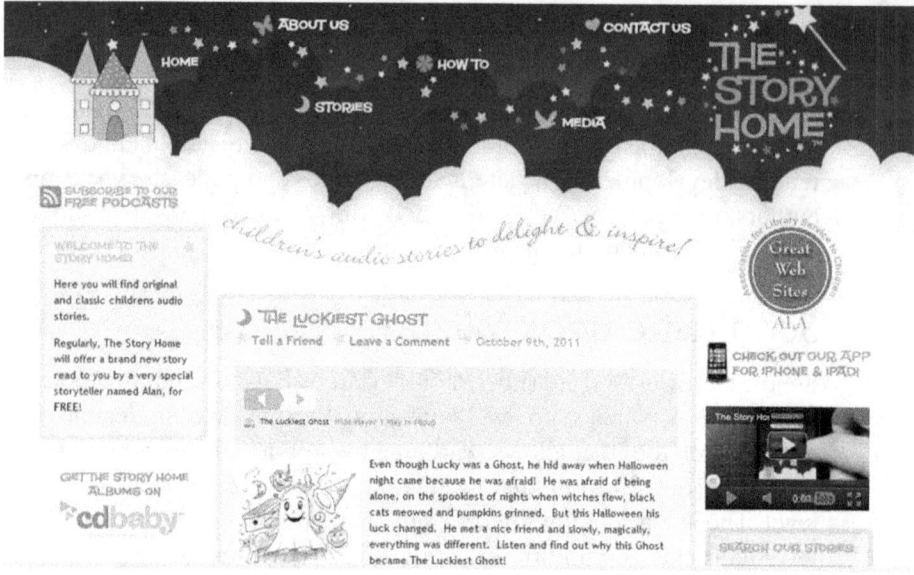

Used with permission of Storyhome.com

The Story Home

The Story Home (www.thestoryhome.com) is a free site that provides podcasts of classic children's literature in public domain. This award-winning site is engaging to students and works online, through a mobile app, through purchased CDs, and with an iPod. Podcasts can be streamed from the site or downloaded for future use.

Other Popular Tools

Other tools, even those with no clear link to books and libraries, can have an application in a 21st-century library media program, as students may be familiar with them and school librarians can easily adapt them to fit into their programs.

Animations (2D and 3D moving characters): ABCya, Photofunny, Xtranormal, Goanimate, Toondoo, Animoto, Toonboom studio. Examples of uses in school library media program: school news, library blogs, wikis, and websites, instructional activities, engaging previews and reviews, announcements, eye-catching messages.

Anime (Japanese-style animation featuring big-eyed characters with often exaggerated body proportions): Zwinky, Gaia dream, Hero Machine, Portrait Machine, Createmypicture. Examples of uses in school library media program: used in creating educational gaming, avatars for web personna, designing characters for writing, reading promotion, signage.

Audio editors (a program that allows multiple audio tracks to be assimilated into a single audio file): Myna, Audioexpert, Audacity. Examples of uses in a school library media program: creating instructional video background sound track, school news shows, kiosk presentations.

Avatars (digital characters that represent one's presence online; can range from a realistic representation to a fantasy): Avatar.Pho.to. Examples of uses in school library media program: website and blog images, student projects, book reviews, digital book talks.

Blogs (interactive web presence for personal and professional publishing): Wordpress, Edublogs, Typepad. Examples of use in school library media program: program web presence, communication and collaboration with patrons and colleagues, posting student work, news and activities updates.

Cartoons and comics (2D still and animated characters): Toondoo, Toon Boom, Disney Toon (http://disney.go.com/games/#/create/), Disney ToonTown (http://toontown.go.com/), Toonzone, Comiclife (www.macinstruct.com/node/69), Readwritethink comic creator (www.readwritethink.org/files/resources/interactives/comic/). Examples of uses in school library media program: attention-getters for instructional, news blurbs, kiosk presentations, graphic novel promotion, student writing and publishing projects, book fair ads.

Course management (Online password-protected classroom interface): rcampus, Moodle. Examples of uses in school library media program: professional learning, staff development, online instruction, patron database and catalog access training.

Digital storytelling (editing program for creating a digital story): Voicethread, Animoto, Yackpack; all presentation links below. Examples of uses in school library media program: school news shows, student projects, web sites, book trailers, vodcasts, kiosk information.

Document sharing (online repository, editing, and sharing site for creating text documents, presentations, and more): Google Docs, Docstoc, Writeboard. Examples of uses in school library media program: collaborative planning.

File converters (convert downloaded files into compatible format for blogs, wikis, websites, and for use in instruction): Real Player, Zamzar. Examples of uses in school library media program: school news, instruction, kiosks, closed-circuit messages.

Graphic organizers (visual representation of topics in a digital product): Gliffy, Webspiration. Examples of uses in school library media program: creating pathfinders, introducing instructional content, organizing subject headings, patron research purposes.

Media hosting (sites for saving files online, especially student projects related to a theme or large files such as multimedia): Voicethread, Picasa, Flickr, Tubes. Examples of uses in school library media program: saving related student projects as for a particular theme, subject area, grade level or class, providing advertising free access to pre-selected media files for students to use in multimedia projects, storing related files from events such as conferences, fairs, and contests.

Microblogs (short message posting to a group of followers): Edmodo, Twitter. Examples of uses in school library media program: send alerts to patrons such as students, parents, and faculty, such as calendar changes, receipt of new materials, assignments, and other brief messages.

Online meetings (interactive two-way communication for two or more users): Skype, Dimdim, Google Voice. Examples of uses in school library media program: author interviews, collaborative projects.

Presentations (digital animated slide show): Prezi, Google Presentations, Slideshare, Sliderocket, Slide.com. Examples of uses in school library media program: instruction, preview and review of content, kiosk with directions, promotions, events listing, digital storytelling.

Rubrics (digital online assessment tools in weighted checklist format): Irubric. Examples of uses in school library media program: instructional assessments, program assessment, course management applications.

Scrapbooking (posting a variety of media to a page): Scrapblog, Glogster, Wix, Wallwisher, 280 Slides, Springnote, Dabbleboard, Smilebox, Flipbook, Shapecollage, Creately, photoVisi. Examples of uses in school library media program: multimedia documentation of program, digital dossier.

Screen capture (produces a video recording of on-screen activity): Screencast-o-matic, Screencast, Jing. Examples of uses in school library media program: useful in creating training videos; can be played back in a kiosk to demonstrate catalog access or database access for patrons; can be used for online staff development or other training or instructional purposes in absence of live instructor.

Social bookmarking (online repository for collection of websites): Delicious, Diigo. Examples of uses in school library media program: sharing favorite websites with patrons and others; allows for categorizing, annotating, and assigning keywords for searching to sites.

Social cataloging (shared catalog of books): LibraryThing, Good Reads, Shelfari. Examples of uses in school library media program: online catalog access, sharing resources, collaboration with other schools and community.

Social map tool (digital tool or widget indicating location of site visitors): Frappr, Clustrmaps, Socialmap, Google Maps. Examples of uses in school library media program: plotting global audience, virtual field trips, Read Across America Week, Flat Stanley travels.

Surveys and polls (online survey and data collection tool): Exemplary sites: Survey Gizmo, SurveyMethods, Survey Monkey, Zoomerang, Vizu, Google Forms: Examples of uses in school library media program: polling patrons; data collection for pre- and post-assessments; voting for favorite authors, books, needs assessment for programs.

Text to speech (animates recorded or typed messages with digital avatars; engaging and motivating to students and other library users): Voki, Blabberize. Examples of uses in school library media program: Engaging presentations; school news; web postings; attention-getters for instructional purposes, key ideas, news, use of another voice to catch patrons' attention or broadcast important points.

Video editing (production of digital video with special effects and transitions): Animoto, Moviemaker Live, Go Animate, Xtranormal. Examples of uses in school library media program: introduction and review of content, presentations, school news, kiosk, infomercials.

Web sites (web presence in CSS format): Wix, Weebly, Facebook, Google Sites. Examples of uses in school library media program: web presence for program; access anytime, anywhere rather than from local intranet.

Wikis (Websites with user editing capability): PBworks, Google Sites, Wikispaces. Examples of uses in school library media program: collaborative writing, pathfinders, library media homepage, discussion boards.

Word clouds (contemporary display of words from a selection of text in order of their prominence in the text. Size of the word display indicates its relationship to the theme; the more frequently a word is repeated, the larger or darker the text in the word cloud): Wordle, ABCya, Worditout. Examples of uses: introducing curriculum content, subject headings in cataloging, contemporary signage, web postings, focus on selections from literature.

Implications for School Librarians

The future of school libraries may be uncertain in these times of budget slashing and job cuts, but one thing is certain: Web 2.0 is gaining ground and cannot be ignored. School librarians can no longer afford to have 20th-century library programs with 21st-century learners. Today's students are at risk without training in 21st-century information literacy and technology literacy skills. Today's students are even more at risk without training in digital citizenship. School libraries must embrace a School Library 2.0 framework in order to best meet the needs of the next generation and help prepare the next generation for the 21st-century workforce.

Action Steps

- School librarians should seek out leaders in their fields who have embraced school library 2.0 and learn from them.
- School librarians should find at least one Web 2.0 tool to master and put into practice in their programs.
- School librarians should create a digital presence for themselves and their school library programs.
- School librarians should network with others who are at approximately the same skill level and challenge each other to stretch beyond their present level.
- School librarians should share what they are doing with others in their field, particularly if they are using Web 2.0 regularly for instruction.

Final Thoughts

It should be shocking to find that school librarians, the very ones who frequently lead in technology innovations, are falling behind in adopting Web 2.0 tools into instruction. At the same time, students are accessing Web 2.0 sites on their own devices, often without supervision or direction in ethical use or digital citizenship. Developing expertise with social media and Web 2.0 tools can no longer be ignored. As district leadership takes more and more control of school networks, and technology support positions are eliminated, local school personnel sometimes fail to recognize the wake-up call. School librarians must embrace this growing trend as a challenge to assume a leadership role in modeling and training faculty and students on Web 2.0 tools and digital citizenship. The next chapter will detail the research-based barriers to Web 2.0 adoption and secret reasons behind such barriers.

Extending the Conversation

Join the online discussion at http://secretreasons.wikispaces.com/.

Subscribe to the wiki's RSS feed to be notified when new discussion posts appear.

1. Is your school library catalog online?
2. If you have an online catalog, what program are you using?
3. If you do not have an online catalog, why not? What obstacles are you facing?
4. What features of Web 2.0 are available in your school library?
    - Chat/IM?
    - Video streaming?
    - Tagging/commenting/rating resources?
    - Digital tutorials?
    - Other. Explain.
5. What tools from the list would you like to know more about?
6. What other tools should be added to the list for school libraries?
7. In what other ways could school librarian programs become more user-centric?
8. What should school librarians do in a district where most of the Web 2.0 tools mentioned are blocked?

School Librarian Handout: Web 2.0 Tools for School Librarians and Readers to Use Now!

Site Name	URL	Features
The Book Seer	http://bookseer.com/	Free interactive readers' advisory, engaging, curious, fun
Book Talk	www.booktalk.org/	Collaborative book discussion with live author chats, publisher and book links, games
Book Trailers-Movies for Literacy	www.homepages.dsu.edu/mgeary/booktrailers/default.htm	300 video book reviews includes elementary
Book Winks	http://bookwink.com/	Award-winning video book review site
Digital Booktalk	http://digitalbooktalk.com/	100 video book reviews for teen and young adult books
Goodreads	www.goodreads.com/	Free social cataloging site; quotes, trivia, listopia
Google Books	http://books.google.com/	Free previews of millions of digitized books and magazines
Google LitTrips	www.googlelittrips.org/	Free bookmapping site; works with Google Earth
International Children's Digital Library	http://en.childrenslibrary.org/	Free digital children's books in 55 languages with multiple search strategies
LibraryThing	www.librarything.com	Free social cataloging with personal bookshelf widget
Online Books Page	http://onlinebooks.library.upenn.edu	One million digitized books, including children's, plays, poetry, periodicals
Reading Rockets	www.readingrockets.org	Free site promoting reading with videos, podcasts, books/authors, quizzes, guides
Scholastic Book Wizard	www.bookwizard.scholastic.com/tbw/homePage.do	Free book leveling tool with multiple search strategies; includes free widget
Shelfari	www.shelfari.com	Free cataloging from Amazon; features NY Times bestseller lists, quotes, virtual bookshelf
The Story Home	www.thestoryhome.com	Free podcasts of classic children's literature; streaming or downloads; colorful, engaging

Permissible to reproduce for educational purposes

From *The Secret Reasons Why Teachers Are Not Using Web 2.0 Tools and What School Librarians Can Do about It* by Peggy Milam Creighton. Santa Barbara, CA : Libraries Unlimited. Copyright © 2012.

CHAPTER 4

Interpreting the Research

Interpretations of research statistics on the use of Web 2.0 tools in K–12 education can explain the secret reasons why Web 2.0 is underutilized, both in instruction and collaboration. In addition, these interpretations of the research can lead to implications for 21st-century school library media specialists who wish to effect positive social change in their schools. These interpretations will be introduced in this chapter, along with implications such interpretations provide for practitioners in the school library media field. Subtopics for this chapter include:

- Interpretation of research results on Web 2.0 use in education.
- Implications from current research for school librarians.

School librarians have traditionally been some of the first to implement new technologies in their school and are often the technology leaders in their schools. At the same time, school librarians may have opportunities to observe situations that school administrators may not. I, for example, have had classroom teachers ask me to do lessons with technology that they felt they were not skilled enough to present themselves. Others have asked me to find out why certain websites are blocked from use at school and what can be done about it. Such situations are frustrating and point to the need for school librarians to model best practices with technology integration, and particularly, Web 2.0 tools. If you have encountered something similar in your school or district, you may be wondering:

- Is it possible for a school library to use Web 2.0 tools when the school or system is not on board?
- What barriers to Web 2.0 use are often faced in school libraries?
- What reasons do teachers frequently give for not using Web 2.0?
- What does current research say about Web 2.0 in school libraries?

If these questions have entered your mind while reading, this chapter is for you! Be sure to join the online discussion by posting your response to the questions at the end of this chapter!

Research on Web 2.0 in 21st-Century Schools

Many school systems have discovered that Web 2.0 tools such as blogging, social networking, and collaborative authoring software can help create participatory learning environments—but the gap between schools that have embraced these tools and those that have not is still large. According to *eSchool News,* the number of schools that are using Web 2.0 tools for instruction remain in the minority (Schools Still Conflicted, 2010).

Willingham (2008), author of *Why Don't Students Like School,* reported on his *Encyclopedia Brittanica* blog that Web 2.0 will definitely not be an integral part of K–12 schools because the idea that collaboration only occurs online is a false assumption. Moreover, direct instruction, as opposed to computer-based instruction, is easier to align with curriculum standards. In fact, Willingham claimed that technology has failed to revolutionize teaching, as its proponents claim, and rather, has cost billions while not bringing about any significant difference in student achievement. The reason, Willingham states, is that the push to integrate technology has really been a response to a series of fads, and support for the various initiatives has been lacking. At the same time, barriers to fully integrating technology have not been eliminated. What are these barriers?

Research-based Reasons Teachers Are Not Using Web 2.0

While they may fall under different categories or different names, the excuses are all somewhat similar to the following:

- Lack of time
- Lack of training
- Lack of tech support
- School culture
- Lack of incentives to integrate technology
- Age of faculty
- Personal characteristics

What the Excuses Really Mean

Excuses may vary from teacher to teacher, but the end result is the same. Whatever the excuse may be, it is often simply a cover-up for the real reason behind the failure to integrate technology into instruction. The following excuses appeared in the research repeatedly with a variation or two on the same theme. Each time, the real reason behind the excuse was slightly different from the excuse given. In each of the sections below is an explanation of what the excuses really mean.

Lack of Time

Lack of time is the number-one excuse for not integrating technology into instruction, particularly Web 2.0 tools. No one can deny that teachers are extremely busy and that the demands on a teacher's time are greater than ever before. Busy teachers have to squeeze in enough time each day ensure that students cover the curriculum standards. Addressing the curriculum standards has a direct link to scoring well on standardized tests and making Adequate Yearly Progress. Since technology standards are not widely included on standardized tests, according to Holland's (2005) article in *Tech Learning,* some teachers may wonder why they should bother.

Research indicates, however, that integrating technology can make a difference in student engagement. Engaging students in learning can be a time-saver for teachers who struggle to keep instruction motivating and relevant to 21st-century student needs and interests. Engagement is key to instruction in all content areas. Instruction in every subject can be more engaging to students when technology resources are integrated into the lesson, particularly interactive Web 2.0 content.

If the excuse for not using Web 2.0 is "not enough time," it really means learning Web 2.0 is not a priority item. How are priorities determined?

Johnson (2007) said that what is measured becomes the priority item. What is required and what is pleasurable generally attains a higher priority than things that require time and energy to master. If introduced to Web 2.0 tools that teachers feel they cannot teach without, they will learn to master them and to make them a priority in their daily instruction.

A lack of time may also mean that teachers feel too pressured to allow for mistakes and exploration while incorporating technology into instruction. Teachers must feel a certain level of comfort before they are willing to step in front of a classroom to teach others, especially older students. New technologies require new skill sets, and new skill sets take time to master fully. Even when teachers are confident of their skills, mastery level requires that teachers devote time to practice Web 2.0 technologies—time that may come at the expense of other activities, such as lesson planning, grading, conferencing with parents, and spending time with family and friends. Often, such mastery also requires additional training, which leads to the next barrier.

Lack of Training

If training is lacking or difficult to come by, it is frequently an excuse for not integrating technology into instruction. No one wants to appear dumb in front of co-workers, peers, and students. It is easier to avoid that which is difficult. Certainly with budgets cuts and position eliminations in many districts, technology training may have fallen by the wayside, and funding for conferences and seminars where training may be acquired may have disappeared entirely.

While lack of training may be a plausible excuse in today's economy, it may also be a sign of something more personal. With the preponderance of online training tools such as podcasts, online courses, and screencasts, the lack of training excuse often means that a teacher lacks motivation to learn on his or her own. In a wired world, lack of training should not be an obstacle. Anyone who wants to learn how to use a Web 2.0 tool can find a free tutorial online or a digital video providing basic instructions for use. Teachers who are motivated to learn can ask someone who already uses that tool to show them how to use it, too. Motivated teachers will find a way to learn to use the tools they value. Sometimes, it simply takes an interested student to motivate his teacher to acquire the training needed.

Teachers who are eager to incorporate new technologies into instruction can also pair up with a buddy teacher who is experienced with that technology. Collaboration with others is a great way to acquire needed skills while still exposing students to meaningful technology experiences.

Sometimes the lack of training means that a teacher has experimented but hit a roadblock and cannot proceed further. The roadblock can be lack of knowledge but more often it is a plugin or software issue that requires tech support. When teachers are not given administrative rights to the computers they use for instruction, it can be too time-consuming or too frustrating to wait for a plug-in to be installed or an update for a site to work properly. Faced with such an obstacle, many teachers simply give up. The technical roadblocks teachers face leads to the next barrier.

Lack of Tech Support

Similar to the complaint about lack of training is the grumbling about lack of tech support. Tech support is critical for maintaining a robust network and for troubleshooting little problems before they get to be big ones. As many school districts have trimmed budgets to the maximum, tech support personnel have been forced onto the chopping block along with other non-instructional positions. A lack of tech support can mean that teachers must be creative in overcoming problems with troubleshooting, technology repairs, and training.

When teachers complain about lack of tech support, what they really mean is that they are afraid to experiment with fixing technical issues themselves. They may have had a bad experience trying to repair a computer themselves or they may be leery of letting someone else help them with a problem. Some may even fear a reprisal if a problem is reported.

However, tech support is not always dependent upon hired experts. Students and staff members may be trained to troubleshoot technology. Users may also be trained to stop problems before they get to be big ones. My personal computer, for example, is equipped with a few technology troubleshooting programs that I run on a regular basis. Staff can be required to run the same programs on their computers, say, once a month. Students can be trained to install printer drivers or reformat hard drives infected with a virus. Even tech-savvy parents can be used as volunteers. School districts such as in the Hillsborough County School District in Florida (citeseerx.ist.psu.edu/viewdoc/download?doi=10.1.1.124.9668) can save thousands of dollars using manpower they have on hand for tech support.

However, a bigger problem than lack of tech support can be the school culture.

School Culture

A common reason for not integrating technology is school culture. School culture designates the focus of instruction in the school and the school improvement goals. School culture determines where and how staff development dollars are spent and what the focus of staff development will be. School culture determines whether or not a school is technology based, literacy based, performing arts based, or a magnet for math and science, for example. If teachers complain about school culture preventing them from integrating technology, they have identified one truth: school culture is pervasive. However, all school focuses can benefit from technology integration, whether the focus is literacy, performing arts, math, science, or technology.

When teachers use school culture as an excuse for not integrating technology, they really mean they do not want to rock the proverbial boat and be a leader or change agent in their schools. They are more comfortable maintaining the status quo. The status quo may be comfortable for a while, but it may also mean that students are missing out on technology skills they must learn to be competitive in today's workforce. It may also mean that lessons are less than engaging, and that expensive and valuable resources may be ignored in favor of tried and true methodologies and resources.

What determines school culture? School culture is comprised of many factors. Parents, community, school history, local history, geography, and students themselves help to determine the school culture. Traditions are a large part of school culture, although traditions can and do change. Traditions include customs, ceremonies, procedures, routines, and events that are practiced repeatedly at specific dates and times. Traditions may dictate the policies that have been in place for some time and can be a major part of school culture. Traditions may also explain the next barrier.

Lack of Incentives to Integrate Technology

When faced with multiple obstacles to technology integration, busy and stressed teachers need a powerful incentive. They need a reason to make an extra effort. Time is already at a premium and lesson planning and grading must still be accomplished. With the demands they already face on meeting curriculum standards, conferencing with parents, and still managing to do everyday tasks, it is little wonder that teachers are less than enthused about going above and beyond.

When teachers complain that there is no incentive to integrate technology into instruction, they are really saying that they are not intrinsically motivated to try technology integration on their own. They will work for a reward such as recognition or the principal's approval, but they are not willing to make the move without something to gain by doing so.

When faced with multiple obstacles, teachers need more than reassurance to try again—they need a powerful incentive. Rewarding those teachers who do integrate technology successfully could be inexpensive and easy to implement. For example, administrators could give the most innovative teachers an extra week off bus duty or an early out one day. They could give recognition in front of peers, also, announcing the teachers' names at staff meetings, on the school announcements, or on the school web page. Administrators could also give awards to teachers on awards day in much the same way that awards are given to top students. Principals might create a Who's Who among the local faculty or post photos on a prominent bulletin board. Other incentives might include extra office supplies, an extra planning period when a sub can be arranged, or even more. If PTA is willing, funds might be allocated to purchase prizes, such as gift cards, salon visits, and so on. Some of these may not be effective incentives, however, if the faculty are veterans nearing retirement.

Age of Faculty

Age of faculty should never be used as an excuse for an educator to fail to learn new skills. Nevertheless, age is frequently cited as an excuse for not integrating technology into instruction. Veteran teachers may say they have learned enough already or that they have been successful doing the same things they have always done. Some may even jokingly adopt the adage, "You can't teach an old dog new tricks," and claim they are old dogs who are too old to learn anything new.

Being near retirement myself, I can honestly claim that no one is too old to learn new tricks, especially teachers. I have never bought into the digital natives/digital immigrants mindset that claims our generation consists of digital immigrants because we did not grow up with computers. On the contrary, being from the transistor radio generation, I think it is our generation that can be called the digital natives. It was transistors, after all, that were the crucial element in the development of the personal computer! It was the transistor radio generation that carried around our portable pre-computing communication devices. Our generation adopted the reel-to-reel tape recorders and the 8-track tape players. Our generation bought the cassette players and Walkmans. Our generation realized the potential for mainframe computers to be reduced in size. Our generation may not have grown up with personal computers, but we were the first to use PCs and teach students to use them. We were also the ones to embrace each new developments in the computing industry. Older teachers, therefore, are likely to be the best equipped to embrace new technologies and teach others to do so, as well.

If teachers claim they are too old to embrace any new technologies, they really mean they are afraid of change—afraid that their teaching styles might no longer be effective and they are afraid of how much they need to learn to meet student needs. Change always requires some risk and the potential for failure. Change can also be renewing and refreshing. The individuals who embrace change will find that they are more flexible and adaptable and are less easily "broken" by a strong winds of change. Perhaps age is a lesser problem compared to the next barrier.

Personal Characteristics

If teachers say they have their own personal reasons for not integrating technology into instruction, they may have a combination of any or all of the above characteristics holding them back. A combination of any or all of the above barriers may account for a nonspecific fear of failure. Teachers who lack time to learn, who do not have training or support when needed, who are not supported by their administrators, or who have little incentive to learn new skills may have a fear of venturing into unknown territory, even if they know the benefits it will have for student achievement. Numerous studies indicate that teachers who have greater skills with technology are less afraid to venture out and try new technologies as well as integrate new technologies into instruction.

Table 4.1: Real Meanings behind the Barriers to Web 2.0 Integration into Instruction

Research-based Barrier	Real Meaning
Lack of time	Learning not a priority
Lack of training	Integration hit a roadblock
Lack of tech support	Afraid to try to fix problems
School culture	Not willing to go against tradition
Lack of incentive	Not intrinsically motivated
Age of faculty	Fear of change
Personal characteristics	Fear of failure

Implications for Practice

The research-based reasons for not integrating technology into instruction, and particularly for not integrating Web 2.0 into instruction, and the real reasons behind these reasons provide a number of implications for school library media specialists who wish to make a positive impact in their fields. First of all, 21st-century school librarians should begin by trying to identify the excuses that prevail in their home schools or districts. Understanding comes about through conversations with individuals and through data-gathering. By asking their co-workers what their beliefs and fears are, school librarians can start assessing the extent of the problem on their own turf.

Next, school librarians should realize that the excuses are not roadblocks. Excuses for not adopting Web 2.0 technologies are simply that—excuses. It is time to put the excuses aside and find a way to embrace Web 2.0 for what it can bring to the classroom. Our students must be taught how to collaborate and create online safely and ethically in order to be effective digital citizens. They must be taught the appropriate ways to interact socially online and at the same time realize the implications of their online activities.

Finally, school librarians must understand that they can make an impact on positive social change. School librarians can play a key role in moving their schools forward with Web 2.0. They can assume a role of leader and change agent in their schools and model safe digital behaviors for their fellow faculty members and for their students. They can advocate for safe integration of Web 2.0 sites that are both engaging and curriculum-related. They can assist students in locating, evaluating, and using information resources and in becoming information literate. Such a role should not be underestimated. In fact, in the rapidly changing digital society, the role of school library media specialists in identifying, evaluating, and instructing in information and technology literacy is more crucial than ever.

Change is never easy. School librarians who wish to move their schools forward should make small changes and realize that each one may take time to fully accomplish. The following action steps suggest a plan for making the move to Web 2.0 integration. The timeline for accomplishing these may vary from school to school and from district to district, depending upon the circumstances at each location, the time available, the administrative support, the condition of the network and technology resources, and the leadership of the school librarian.

Action Steps

- School librarians should build time into their schedules for learning Web 2.0 skills; they might begin with a site such as 23 Things or Cool Tools 4 Schools and master one step at a time.
- School librarians should offer training to others on the skills they have mastered.
- School librarians should assist tech-savvy students in becoming tech support assistants at their local schools, offering help to peers and teachers as needed.
- School librarians should work with their principals to help alleviate fear of change by presenting engaging tools for teachers to learn in a safe environment—during a staff meeting, for example, or at a curriculum planning meeting.
- School librarians should work with their principals to offer incentives to staff who are willing to be the team tech leaders for their halls or grade levels; small tokens such as takeaways from conferences, coupons, free books, and other goodies will go a long way in reinforcing positive behaviors

Extending the Conversation

Join the online discussion at http://secretreasons.wikispaces.com/.

Subscribe to the wiki's RSS feed to be notified when new discussion posts appear.

1. What barriers to technology integration exist in your school or district?
2. How do you feel about barriers to technology integration in your school or district?

3. Is time a barrier to technology integration in your school? If so, what time issues have you faced and how have you overcome it? Explain.
4. Is technology training a barrier to technology integration in your school? Do you have technology training available? If so, who provides it?
5. Is lack of administrative support a barrier to technology integration in your school? If not, does the administration support technology integration? Explain. If so, what can be done about it?
6. Describe your school culture. Is the culture of your school supportive of technology integration or is it a barrier to technology integration? Explain.
7. Are you personally integrating Web 2.0 into your program?
8. What do you believe is the greatest barrier to technology integration?

Teacher Handout: Overcoming Barriers to Web 2.0 Integration into Instruction

Research-based Barrier	**Real Meaning**	**Resources**
Lack of time	Learning Web 2.0 is not a priority	http://techpp.com/2011/01/26/top-12-web-2-0-sites-for-teachers/
		www.slideshare.net/langwitches/70-tools-70-minutes?src=related_normal&rel=3739281
Lack of training	Integration hit a roadblock	www.internet4classrooms.com/on-line.htm
		www.teacher2teacher.com/
Lack of tech support	Afraid to try to fix problems	www.techguy.org/
		www.askdrtech.com/
School culture	Not willing to go against tradition	www.nais.org/publications/ismagazinearticle.cfm?ItemNumber=150099
		www.sedl.org/change/school/culture.html
Lack of incentive	Not intrinsically motivated	www.ncrel.org/sdrs/areas/issues/methods/technlgy/te200.htm
		http://fno.org/sum99/reluctant.html
Age of faculty	Fear of change	http://scholarcommons.usf.edu/cgi/viewcontent.cgi?article=3390&context=etd&sei-redir=1#search=%22age%20faculty%20technology%20use%22
Personal characteristics	Fear of failure	http://wsfcsnewteachertips.blogspot.com/2011/03/dont-let-fear-of-failure-stand-in-way.html
		www.organizational-change-management.com/organizational-change-and-resistance.php

From *The Secret Reasons Why Teachers Are Not Using Web 2.0 Tools and What School Librarians Can Do about It* by Peggy Milam Creighton. Santa Barbara, CA : Libraries Unlimited. Copyright © 2012.

CHAPTER 5

How School Librarians Can Serve as Change Agents in Their Schools

This chapter will provide numerous strategies for school librarians to implement in order to serve as change agents for modeling Web 2.0 use in their schools and for instructing other educators to do so, as well. The chapter will include numerous web-based resources, including an online training course, a blog for posting thoughts and comments, a wiki for sharing projects, rubrics for assessment, and more. Subtopics include:

- The plan
- Additional strategies
- Web-based resources: online course, blog, wiki, rubric

The school library media profession is at a crossroads. No longer are school librarians in a position safe from budget cuts. School librarians must assume the role of leaders who are relevant and viable in their schools, or face the same chopping block that has eliminated other positions. School librarians who stay on the cutting edge of best practices, who stay abreast of research and technology-based skills, and who teach other professionals to do the same are invaluable in their schools. They will be much less likely to face cuts if their administrators, directors, and school boards see them as crucial members of the staff and team players. As such, school librarians can leverage their leadership roles to become change agents who advocate for the benefits of integration of Web 2.0 tools into 21st-century instruction.

- Are you committed to your profession enough to advocate for change?
- Who else do you know that serves as a change agent in your school or district?
- Are you a change agent in your school or district?
- Why is it important for school librarians to assume the role of change agent in their schools or districts?
- What can school librarians do to effect positive social change on the job and in their professional networks?

If you have ever asked yourself any of these questions, or if you are just becoming aware of the possibilities for positive social change through your contacts, this chapter is for you. Be sure to join the discussion and post your thoughts to the questions at the end of this chapter.

The Setting

You are evaluating your school library media program, and want to make it as relevant to your patrons as possible. You are committed to embracing 21st-century tools and integrating Web 2.0 into your instructional program. You have evaluated the pros and cons and you have identified the barriers you might face. Can you influence others in your school to get on board with you? If you have decided you want to make a positive change toward embracing Web 2.0 technologies, this chapter is for you!

If you are have admitted that change is needed in your school or district, and if you have recognized any of the barriers to Web 2.0 adoption listed in previous chapters, but did not know how to make a positive difference, the next section will detail a seven-step plan for change. Even if you do not follow all of the steps in the plan, you are still making a positive difference. If you take the first step, changes will begin to happen. If you complete the plan, change is inevitable.

The Seven-Step Plan

Step 1: Analyze the Standards

The first step in effecting change within your program is to analyze the standards. At first glance, this may seem a relatively simple task, but media specialists have multiple standards to consider. First of all, curriculum standards should be the baseline for program evaluation. You could use your district or state department of education's technology curriculum standards, or you could analyze your program against the national Common Core Standards (www.corestandards.org/the-standards).

Next, you might consider the American Association of School Librarians standards for the 21st-century learner (http://bit.ly/csCNCG) and the International Society for Technology in Education's National Educational Technology Standards (www.iste.org/standards.aspx).

Finally, you might consider analyzing your program against the accreditation standards for your school, district, or state, such as www.advanc-ed.org/standards.

Now you are ready to get a comprehensive snapshot of where your program stands in relationship to the standards. A number of high-quality products exist for measuring programs, such as the Michigan 21 (www.michigan.gov/documents/mde/lm_SL21_313134_7.pdf) or the NY State Education Dept. rubric (www.p12.nysed.gov/technology/library/SLMPE_rubric/documents/SLMPE_rubric.pdf).

After considering curriculum, program, and accreditation standards carefully, you should be in a position to study the level of technology integration you are practicing yourself, as well as the level of technology integration at your school.

Step 2: Assess Where You Are in Adopting Web 2.0 Technology Tools into Instruction

A number of tools might be useful in analyzing the level of technology integration in your school or district, or analyzing your personal level of technology integration. One of easiest tools to use is the Florida Technology Integration Matrix (http://fcit.usf.edu/matrix/index.html) and it is free! The Levels of Technology Integration (LoTi) survey is recently updated to include digital-age technologies.

LoTi is very well known and widely accepted, but requires a paid membership to access.

Step 3: Explore Tools That Meet Your Needs

The tools listed in the first four chapters of this book are a great starting point for exploration but, there are many more. Begin a search by looking for a tool to serve a specific purpose, such as "video editing," "presentation," or "document sharing." To your search terms, add qualifiers such as "free," "online," "education," and perhaps "best" or "top 10." Experiment with one or two that seem to meet your needs and become familiar with them. Create a project of some sort using the new tool and save or embed it on a blog, wiki, or website. Use your project as a model to teach others how to use the same tool. Create a slide show, screencast, or even a text document of directions and recommendations for using your newfound tool. Save your work for future training sessions.

Step 4: Create a Personal Plan for Action

Work closely with your school library committee, technology committee, school improvement committee, team leaders, or other leaders in your school to create a local school action plan. Your action plan should define the technology and curriculum standards you are addressing, the administrators of the plan, the resources needed, the budget, the timeline, and the assessment strategies for your plan. Some of the action plans written by others (see Wisconsin's www.dpi.state.wi.us/imt/doc/libmedchck.doc or Missouri's http://dese.mo.gov/divteachqual/leadership/profdev/LMS.pdf) can be a starting point for you, but these plans should be fine-tuned to meet your specific needs. Work with your committee to make your plan a personal plan that is uniquely suited to your situation.

Step 5: Learn New Skills

A significant part of the plan should include time to learn and master new skills. School librarians can learn on their own or from others. Great content is available online for motivated learners, such as this blog: http://schoollibrarylearning2.csla.net/2007/02/23-things_27.html. Perhaps a share session where teachers and librarians share their favorite Web 2.0 tools could be arranged. A school-wide technology day might also offer an opportunity for teachers and students to get involved as partners sharing their favorite tools and creating an online repository of ideas in a wiki or blog. A Technology Night may allow parents and other community partners to join in, as well. Another idea would be to designate one day per week or one day a month to technology learning. Other schools can be a great source of ideas, as well, such as those listed in the School Library Toolbox: http://sltoolbox.libguides.com/content.php?pid=206072&sid=1718897.

Step 6: Train Others

After acquiring needed skills for yourself, begin to train others to adopt new skills, as well. The early adopters that you train can be helpful in getting other staff on board and offering training to meet the needs of all. Training others also helps you to fine-tune your own skills and formulate answers to questions you may not have conceived while developing your new skills. While training others, you can develop a reputation as an expert, a leader, a take-charge person who can help others. Your training role can be useful in leveraging other leadership roles, such as working with your principal for your school library program goals.

Step 7: Integrate Technology into Instruction

Once you have learned new skills yourself and trained others on those skills, the final step is to integrate those skills into instruction. This is the point where many plans fall short. Teachers learn new skills but never learn ways to integrate them into their instruction, so the tech skills they learned eventually disappear. Create a repository of exciting, engaging activities for your students that integrate a technology standard with a curriculum standard, and you are halfway home. Integrate multiple standards and you will have a winning combination on your hands. Model the technology projects you have created for others to see. Post them on your blogs and wikis and share them at staff meetings and trainings. Offer to share student projects on your school news shows, at district level events, at Technology Nights, conferences, and fairs. Get the word out widely, and it will have a snowball effect that will not disappear.

Scenarios

Analyze where you are in terms of the following scenarios to help determine your next steps.

Scenario 1

Alexis Gleason is a school librarian in a large suburban school district. She has been at the same school for more than 10 years. Since the time she was hired, she has worked closely with her principal to develop a positive working relationship and establish trust. The principal respects her opinion and is willing to listen to her. Alexis has leveraged the strength of their relationship to suggest that she offer technology training to her staff in lieu of the district-wide training that was cut from the budget last year. As she told her principal, she can personalize the training to meet individual teacher needs and customize it to fit into the school improvement plan goals. Her goal, however, is to introduce the teaching staff to some Web 2.0 sites that can be used to improve student writing performance, an area of weakness on the performance-based testing for the past five years. She shows the principal some data on the low test scores and suggests that her role would be to customize a plan of action to meet needs at each individual grade level. She is also going to integrate instruction on the district subscription databases into the teacher training, showing the staff how using the databases can lead students directly to the best data for research projects at each grade level and meet curriculum standards for informational writing. The principal hesitates for a moment, and Alexis suggests that she can meet with the principal ahead of time to get her okay on all that she wants to show the teachers, as well as to collect data on student achievement after the training. The principal likes the plan and gives her the go-ahead. While this is out of the normal course of business for Alexis, she recognizes the opportunity to serve and leverage to power of the training to seek opportunities to collaborate with teachers who have been reluctant to collaborate in the past. She also sees it is a chance to develop her leadership skills and advocate for school library resources. With her principal's blessing, she forges ahead.

- How would you compare yourself to Alexis?
- Have you faced any of the issues she has faced?
- Have you leveraged your leadership role at the local school level?
- Do you conduct any technology training for your staff?
- What can you share from your own personal experiences?

Scenario 2

Jackie Chaffen has been a school librarian for 29 years and is looking forward to retirement. She has seen a lot of changes in her career, including adding computers and computerized databases to the library, and automating the catalog and circulation systems. Jackie has tried to stay abreast of all the changes but feels like she can no longer compete with the younger staff members who are always texting each other and using their smartphones to search the web rather than a computer. One of her pet peeves is that the teachers allow their students to go straight to Google and avoid using the websites she has selected for student research projects, and that they never encourage the students to use the subscription databases. Jackie knows she can push the issue but hesitates to "rock the boat." She has one more year until she retires. She visualizes the free time she has ahead of her and hopes she can coast through next year without any conflict.

- Do you know of some staff members like Jackie?
- Have you been guilty of going straight to Google and avoiding subscription databases?
- How do your students gather information?
- What could be done to work more closely with Jackie and encourage her to promote her knowledge and resources with staff and students?

Influence Beyond the Local School

Can your influence spread beyond the staff at your local school? Yes! School librarians are uniquely positioned to serve as technology leaders and wield a world-wide influence. It is time for school librarians to step up to the plate and leverage their leadership influence to make a significant difference in Web 2.0 adoption for the next generation.

School Librarians as Change Agents

Rogers (1995) and others have called those individuals who influence others change agents. Change agents are often ahead of others in adapting new habits or joining new movements. Because they tend to be well respected, change agents may hold leadership positions within their social groups, making them influential in bringing about social change.

School librarians are well positioned to serve as change agents in their schools. They often meet with their principals and other committees to develop policies and procedures for their school library programs. They meet regularly with team leaders to collaboratively plan instructional activities for students. They supervise library staff members and volunteers and direct Parent-Teacher Association involvement in the library program. They make budgetary and purchasing decisions, and deliver staff development training sessions on issues such as technology and copyright law. School librarians wear many hats in their schools and may have a wide influence on social groups within their schools (Schulz-Jones, 2009). In their capacity as a member of multiple social groups and as a collaborator with faculty, administrators, parents, and community members, school librarians are well suited to serve as change agents in their schools.

School Librarians as Advocates in Their Communities

As change agents for Web 2.0 use, school librarians can wield their influence on administrators, team leaders, teachers, teacher educators, parents, community members, and students in advocating for Web 2.0 use. First, school librarians should present research such as this book provides to their principals, emphasizing the positive impact of Web 2.0 on student achievement in order to obtain administrative support for Web 2.0 integration into instruction.

School librarians could take the most relevant research nuggets and put them into a brief bullet-list flyer, or eye-catching video, and present these to the leaders of the many social groups to which they are members. Parent groups might appreciate a flyer, team leaders might like a bulleted list, teacher educators might respond positively to a journal article, parents might like a short newsletter article, and so on. School librarians could also seek to present comments before their respective school boards. They should regularly post data to any communication medium they choose: blogs, wikis, newsletters, memos, web pages, and more.

In order to gain support of district supervisors and superintendents, school librarians should take advantage of any opportunity to promote the positive results of Web 2.0 integration into instruction, particularly when it shines a positive light on their schools or districts. Community news agencies are excellent channels for spreading the news to partners in education, school boards, parents, community members, and charitable organizations.

School librarians should publicize Web 2.0 integration in their own programs by advertising the programs and activities occurring in their school libraries. Traffic records, reader comments, survey responses and other blog interactions, could serve as evidence-based support for the impact blogging can have on students, faculty and the community. Further support for evidence-based practice could be obtained through wikis that serve as repositories for lesson plans, student work, screencasts and streaming media, program guides. These two tools alone could build a compelling case for Web 2.0 use school-wide.

School Librarians as Technology Trainers

As school librarians begin to leverage their influence, they can change hats seamlessly. One hat that I particularly advocate for school librarians to wear regularly is that of technology trainer. As leaders in integrating technology resources into instruction, school librarians can model exemplary collaborative projects as well as develop ways to serve as technology trainers on Web 2.0 tools for collaboration. Outstanding collaborative projects can then be published on wikis, blogs, and streaming media for training. School librarians can create other training tools for everyday practice, such as online courses and screencasts.

Savvy school librarians might form study groups for the purpose of developing strategies for integrating Web 2.0 at their local school. Reflection, peer observation, modeling exemplary lessons, and other best practices can be used for training tools to jump start Web 2.0 integration at the local school level. Partners in education, PTAs, community supporters, and others can reward early adopters of Web 2.0 integration with benefits such as administrative-approved flex-time, local school recognition, monetary awards, and small gifts.

School Librarians as Models

School librarians can add a definition of Web 2.0 to their e-mail signature or create a streaming video or podcast about what Web 2.0 means and how it benefits student learning. School librarians can speak about Web 2.0 integration into instruction at faculty meetings and post ideas on their blog pages.

Dauntless school librarians should leverage opportunities to exemplify use of Web 2.0 with their co-workers and students. School librarians might design a wiki repository of library 2.0 lesson plans for coworkers to browse. The wiki could also host curriculum-based websites, exemplary student projects, quizzes, standards-based practices. The wiki could serve as evidence of the impact of Web 2.0

instructional activities on student achievement. Wiki visits could be recorded through the use of hit counters, discussion posts, and other indicators of reader participation.

School Librarians as Trendsetters

Similarly, school librarians could become Web 2.0 trendsetters in their local schools. School library blogs could be used to communicate with parents, host surveys, post calendars for scheduling activities, feature research pathfinders, WebQuests, student work, book reviews, newsletters, handbooks, and more. Wikis and blogs could be used to host streaming audio and video, screencasts, IM reference services, and links to online databases and other resources (Hastings, 2008; Maness, 2006). Trendsetting school librarians could then screencast their own tutorials on how to create a pathfinder, access an online resource, post media, blog, create a wiki, and so forth, for the purpose of sharing knowledge with others and thus impacting a greater number of students.

School librarians should eventually seek to publish their efforts in educational journals so that other practitioners may benefit from their expertise.

School Librarians as Teacher Trainers

School librarians should post training modules for Web 2.0 use on social media such as YouTube, TeacherTube, and more. They should create blogs and wikis to deposit their instructional materials and make them freely available for general use. They should tweet about the location of these instructional materials so that others can find them. School librarians should even create their own free courses and course management systems with screencasts, text tutorials, and more.

School Librarians and Classroom Teachers

School librarians should work closely with classroom teachers to help them experiment with the many Web 2.0 tools suggested in this book, and to consider the many ways such tools could be used to improve student achievement in their classrooms.

School librarians should encourage those classroom teachers who become familiar with specific Web 2.0 tools to teach other teachers to use them. Teacher experts wield a great deal of power and can share their best practices within the local school, at staff meetings and professional development sessions. Their influence beyond the local school at district, state, and national educational conferences can help advocate for the use of Web 2.0 integration and removal of barriers to use.

School librarians should assist classroom teachers in creating web-based training tools that can also be shared with the global teaching community so that others can realize the impact that Web 2.0 tools could have on student achievement and engagement in learning activities.

School Librarians and School Culture

It may not be practical to try to change school culture. A wise move would be to weave in a new custom—if it has been a practice at graduation to show photos of graduates, for example, offer to make a more engaging display than a slide show by using Web 2.0 tools. Show how Web 2.0 tools can create a very high-quality display that can be embedded or downloaded and shared.

The leadership of the school can be a major determining factor in establishing school culture. Sometimes school culture can be pervasive and persistent, even with a change in administration. New leadership will often hesitate to make changes at first, but all leaders have their own agenda. Work with the administration as much as possible. Find ways to integrate all the Web 2.0 tools you can. If communication is a priority of your administration, find and learn all the Web 2.0 tools that can be used to communicate more effectively. Share them at staff meetings. Model them with students. Use them often and send links to your staff. Embed in your webpages and blogs. Host projects online. Share at staff development meetings. Brag on staff who use them, too.

School Librarians and Teacher Educators

School librarians can influence future media specialists, as well. Working with area schools of education, school librarians can challenge teacher educators to encourage their undergraduate and graduate students to explore Web 2.0 tools with future faculty members in order to increase the practice of Web 2.0 integration with all school professionals.

School librarians might get a toe hold at the university level by offering to speak to students in schools of education about the importance of working with school librarians and learning from them. They can offer to teach prospective teachers and school librarians some useful Web 2.0 research tools, such as how to use Google advanced search strategies, Google Scholar, and iGoogle, or how to set up their own RSS feeds to deliver pertinent blog posts and news items to their personal start pages.

School librarians might also be able to collaborate with teacher educators to spread the word at educational conferences or publish in educational journals. School librarians could even offer to assist with graduate research agendas or as guest instructors for one class period, sharing their expertise and skills with Web 2.0 research tools with other educators.

School Librarians and School Administrators

School librarians can have a great impact by working with school administrators. One easy way to collaborate is by assisting school administrators in locating the most current research to share at staff meetings on the impact of Web 2.0 integration on student achievement and the ways in which school librarians can integrate Web 2.0 tools effectively to meet the needs of both students and faculty.

School librarians might also assist school administrators in minimizing the barriers to Web 2.0 integration, especially those that have been repeatedly identified in scholarly research (Buzzeo, 2008; Lockerby et al., 2004; Morin, 2008; Todd, 2008) such as lack of time, school culture, faculty resistance, and lack of administrative support, because these factors might be hindering Web 2.0 integration in their own schools. In addition, school librarians should offer to present training sessions on Web 2.0, ways in which the library program can impact student achievement and technology that can save time and allow greater communication and Web 2.0 use in all curricular areas.

School Librarians and Community Partners

School librarians can have a wide influence in their local areas. One means of spreading the work is by working with community members and partners in education to publicize positive results of Web 2.0 use in schools. An effective means of drawing in the community is for school librarians to offer parents training sessions on Web 2.0 use, showing samples of student projects, encouraging parents to become involved with student Web 2.0 use, and offering day and evening courses to help parents become skilled at tools such as blogs, wikis, and sites students might commonly use in completing school work.

Next Steps

Now you are ready to begin transforming your school library media program into a School Library 2.0 program. Share your progress in the journey with others who may be facing the same challenges and obstacles as you are. Learn from others who have gone the same route and been successful. Publish your thoughts to the discussion group or on the wiki. Best wishes!

Extending the Conversation

Join the online discussion at http://secretreasons.wikispaces.com/.

Subscribe to the wiki's RSS feed to be notified when new discussion posts appear.

1. Does your school or district have a technology plan?
2. Is the media specialist considered a technology expert in your school or district?
3. What technology tools or skills are lacking in your school or district?
4. What is the most pressing technology issue in your school or district?
5. Where will you begin with your personal action plan?
6. What technology training tools have you used successfully in the past?
7. What technology training tools have you seen used successfully at conferences or in professional development you have attended?
8. What remains to be done for technology to be fully integrated into instruction in your school or district?

Teacher and School Librarian Handout

Personal Action Plan for (name) _____

Step	Action	Suggested Resources
1	Analyze standards	Common Core Standards (www.corestandards.org/the-standards)
		AASL Standards for the 21st Century Learner (http://bit.ly/csCNCG)
		ISTE NETS (www.iste.org/standards.aspx)
2	Assess where you are	LoTi
		Fl Technology Integration Matrix (http://fcit.usf.edu/matrix.index.html)
3	Explore tools to meet your needs	Begin with suggestions in this book or search a list such as Schrock's
		http://freetech4teachers.com/
4	Create a plan for action	See models such as Wisconsin's (www.dpi.state.wi.us/imt/doc/libmedchck.doc) or MO's http://dese.mo.gov/divteachqual/leadership/profdev/LMS.pdf
5	Learn new skills	23 things
		Atomic Learning
		PD 360
6	Train others	Technology night
		Local school staff development
		District or regional share sessions
		Conference Presentations such as ISTE, AASL, etc.
7	Integrate technology into instruction	Post evidence to your blog or wiki: video, samples of projects, photo streams, presentations, comments

Other Ideas: _____

From *The Secret Reasons Why Teachers Are Not Using Web 2.0 Tools and What School Librarians Can Do about It* by Peggy Milam Creighton. Santa Barbara, CA : Libraries Unlimited. Copyright © 2012.

Glossary

AdWords: Google's advertising campaign designed to promote web traffic through the use of targeted keywords; http://adwords.google.com/support/aw/bin/static.py?hl=en&guide=21899&page=guide.cs.

Ajax: Asynchronous Java Script and XML programming language built to be interactive; causes web pages to update immediately, based upon a user's activity on the site.

Animation: simulated movement of cartoon characters.

Anime: colorful Japanese animation, particularly in the science fiction genre.

API: Application Program Interface.

audio editor: program that allows users to make changes to audio files.

avatar: 2D animated character used as an alter ego for a living being.

Bing: Microsoft's new search engine; www.bing.com.

blog: a weblog or web-based journal.

broadband: a wide band of frequencies able to rapidly transmit a large amount of data.

change agents: individuals who have influence over decisions made by others.

cloud computing: the use of remote networked servers to host programs and store data.

collaboration: the act of working jointly with two or more people.

comment: the process of uploading personal thoughts to another's blog post or website.

connectivism: theory that describes the interconnected online community of learners; www.connectivism.ca/about.html.

constructivism: theory that describes the process of creating knowledge or meaning; www.connectivism.ca/?p=65.

CoSN: Consortium of School Networking; www.cosn.org.

course management: a password-protected site where all components of a course are hosted online, including a course syllabus, assignments, links to resources, and a place for students to connect via chat, IM, asynchronous discussion groups, video chat, and more; for example, Blackboard, Moodle (http://moodle.org/).

CSS: Cascading Style Sheets; a method used to format web page design and layout; www.w3schools.com/css/.

cyber-bullying: the process of sending threatening messages online.

cybertheft: the act of stealing data online.

dial-up: Internet access via a telephone line connection.

digital divide: the gap between those who have technology access and those who do not; www.pewinternet.org/topics/Digital-Divide.aspx.

digital storytelling: the process of creating a digital, or computer-based story, especially personal narratives.

document sharing: providing read or read-write access to an online document for another user.

dynamic: the programming code that causes a website's contents to change based on a user's clicks.

embed: the process of inserting html code so that an external file or widget can be housed within a site.

file converter: a tool used to convert a digital file from one format to another.

filter: a software application that blocks access to specific sites or types of sites.

folksonomy: social organization of information through the use of popular keywords, or tags.

FTP: file transfer protocol; a process used to move files from one computer to another via the Internet.

graphic organizer: a chart, table, diagram, or other visual arrangement of data.

HTML: Hypertext Markup Language; the programming language that allows users to click on a word in order to progress to another linked file.

hyperlink: the act of directing users to a related website or file by clicking on a word or image.

hypertext: a digital file that is connected to another through hyperlinks.

IM: instant messaging.

information literacy: the complex set of skills involved in finding, evaluating, and effectively using information.

LoTi: Levels of Technology Integration survey. Available free at http://www.lqhome.com/cgi-bin/WebObjects/lotilounge.woa.

media literacy: the skills of finding, evaluating, and effectively using information from a variety of media.

microblogs: small posts of approximately 120 characters or less.

multimedia: various types of media such as audio, video, and photos.

photostream: setting up a folder of photos posted online to play one after the other continuously.

podcast: an audio file that can be played online or downloaded to play on a portable listening device such as an iPod or other MP3 player.

pop-up: a small program, usually an advertisement, that is designed to appear in a separate window when a user accesses a website.

RDF: Resource Descriptive Framework; a means of classifying data so that machines can process it semantically; a key component of the Semantic Web

RSS: abbreviation for Really Simply Syndication; a format for content on sites such as blogs and wikis that may be delivered at a user's request through a subscription service such as Google reader and Bloglines, among others.

rubric: a means of assessing a product by ranking specific characteristics that product against exemplars on a scale from low to high.

School Library 2.0 theory: the theory that a school library which embraces Web 2.0 tools in its programming and operations becomes more relevant to 21st-century patrons.

screen capture: a tool that makes a video of computer screen activity.

screenshot: a tool that makes a still photo of a computer screen.

Semantic web: a means of representing data so that computers can process it in a way that is meaningful to humans, such as producing search results based on a user's previous activity

sidebar: the content that appears in the left- or right-hand column of a blog or website.

smartphone: a wireless mobile phone with Internet capability and programming apps.

social capital: the added value that results from user traffic on a blog or website.

socially constructed: created with input from a variety of users.

social map: a map that indicates the location of the visitors to that site.

social media: photos, videos, and music that is widely shared online.

social networking: the process of connecting with other users online.

social networking theory: the study of the impact of social relationships and connections on a network of members.

spam: unwanted or undesirable email; junk mail online.

SPARQL: the programming language of Web 2.0 that allows users to search for information with no knowledge of programming language or code.

sponsor: a paid advertiser that helps to finance the cost of the website.

static: unchanged, as in a webpage that remains the same even after users click on a link posted there.

syndication: providing updated information simultaneously to multiple websites through subscription feeds.

tag: to assign a keyword that describes an online file to help others locate it; for example, adding a descriptive title, name, or place to a photo.

taxonomy: a system of organization.

ubiquitous: everywhere, particularly as referring to Internet access.

URL: Universal Resource Locator, or web address.

viral: wildly popular with an extreme number of "hits."

virtual world: an online simulation.

vodcast: a video broadcast.

webinar: a seminar held on the web.

Web 1.0: the read-only web.

Web 2.0: the read-write web.

widget: a small program with a specific function (such as a clock, weather map, or calendar) that can be embedded on a blog, wiki or webpage.

WiFi: wireless network, as in a school or library.

wiki: a website with the capacity for multiple users to edit.

World Wide Web: the networked resources and users accessing information via the Internet.

XML: acronym for extensible markup language; the language used to configure data on the web pages.

Works Cited

Aharony, N. (2008, January). Web 2.0 in U.S. LIS schools: Are they missing the boat? *Ariadne, 54*. Retrieved from http://www.ariadne.ac.uk/issue54/.

Anderson, C. (2007). Adequate yearly progress at your library media center. *Library Media Connection, 25*(4), 22–24.

Baumbach, D. (2009). Web 2.0 and you. *Knowledge Quest, 37*(4), 12–19.

Berners-Lee, T. (2007). Q&A with Tim Berners-Lee. *Businessweek*. Retrieved from www.businessweek.com/technology/content/apr2007/tc20070409_961951.htm.

Bosco, J., Saltpeter, J., & Mahon-Santos, A. (2010). Web 2.0 as a force for transformation: A tale of six districts. *COSN Compendium 2010, 8*(2). Retrieved from www.cosn.org/Portals/7/docs/compendium/2010/Executive%20Summary/CoSN%20Compendium-%20Web%2020%20as%20Force%20for%20School%20Exec%20Summary.pdf.

Braulein, M. (2008). Turned on, plugged in, online and dumb: Student failure despite the techno revolution. *Encyclopedia Brittannica Blog*. Retrieved from www.britannica.com/blogs/2008/10/turned-on-plugged-in-online-dumb-student-failure-despite-the-techno-revolution/.

Brinkerhoff, J. (2006). Effects of a long-duration, professional development academy on technology skills, computer self-efficacy, and technology integration and beliefs. *Journal of Research on Technology in Education, 39*(1), 22–43.

Brodie, C. (2006, October). Collaboration practices. *School Library Media Activities Monthly, 23*(2), 27–30.

Buzzeo, T. (2008). *The collaboration handbook*. Columbus, OH: Linworth Publishing.

Collier, A. (2010). A better safety net. *School Library Journal, 55*(11), 36–38.

Creighton, P. (2010). *Perceptions of Web 2.0 as catalysts for teacher and librarian collaboration*. Unpublished doctoral dissertation, Walden University.

Dickinson, G. (2010). How do you use social networking tools? *Library Media Connection, 28*(5), 45.

Farkas, M. D. (2007). *Social software in libraries: Building collaboration, communication, and community online.* Medford, NJ: Information Today.

Federal Communications Commission. (2009). *Children's Internet Protection Act: FCC consumer facts.* Retrieved from www.fcc.gov/cgb/consumerfacts/cipa.html.

Hastings, R. (2008, November/December). Collaborating across time zones: How 2.0 technology can bring your global team together. *Information Today,* 16–19.

Holland, J. (2005, December). When teachers don't get it: Myths, misconceptions, and other tardiddle. *Tech Learning.* Retrieved from www.techlearning.com/article/4970.

House passes bill restricting social networking sites. (2006, September). *American Libraries, 37*(8), 9.

Inan, F., & Lowther, D. (2010). Factors affecting technology integration in K–12 classrooms: A path model. *Education Tech Research Development, 58,* 137–154.

Johnson, D. (2007). *What gets measured gets done: A school library media and technology self-study workbook.* Retrieved from www.doug-johnson.com/dougwri/whatgets.pdf.

Lockerby, R., Lynch, D., Sherman, J., & Nelson, E. (2004). Collaboration and information literacy: Challenges of meeting standards when working with remote faculty. *Journal of Library Administration, 41*(1/2), 243–253.

Maness, J. M. (2006). Library 2.0 theory: Web 2.0 and its implications for libraries. *Webology, 3*(2) Article 25. Retrieved from http://www.webology.org/2006/v3n2/a25.html.

Morin, M. (2008). Moving towards collaboration—One step at a time. *School Library Media Activities Monthly, 24*(8), 18–19.

Naslund, J., & Giustini, D. (2008). Towards School Library 2.0: An introduction to social software tools for teacher librarians. *School Libraries Worldwide, 14*(2), 55–68.

O'Reilly, T. (2005). What is Web 2.0?. (blog post). Retrieved from http://oreilly.com/pub/a/web2/archive/what-is-web-20.html?page=1

Partnership for 21st Century Skills. (2009). *Framework for 21st century learning.* Retrieved from vfz/.ehttp://www.p21.org/storage/documents/P21_Framework_Definitions.pdf.

Richardson, W. (2010). *Blogs, wikis, podcasts and other powerful web tools for classrooms.* Thousand Oaks, CA: Corwin Press.

Rogers, E. (1995). *Diffusion of innovations* (4th ed.). New York: The Free Press.

Rowand, C. (2000). *Teacher use of computers and Internet in public schools.* United States Department of Education Institute of Education Sciences' National Center for Education Statistics. Retrieved from http://nces.ed.gov/pubs2000/2000090.pdf.

Schools still conflicted over Web 2.0 tools. (2010). *eSchool News.* Retrieved from www.eschoolnews.com/2010/09/28/schools-still-conflicted-over-web-2-0-tools/.

Schulz-Jones, B. (2009). Collaboration opportunities in the school social network. *Knowledge Quest, 37*(4), 20–25.

Shannon, V. (2006, May 23). A more revolutionary web. *New York Times* (Technology). Retrieved from www.nytimes.com/2006/05/23/technology/23iht-web.html.

Todd, R. (2008). Collaboration: From myth to reality: Let's get down to business. Just do it! *School Library Media Activities Monthly, 24*(7), 54–58.

Trotter, A. (2007, September 12). Digital divide 2.0. *Education Week*. Retrieved from www.edweek.org/dd/articles/2007/09/12/02divide.h01.html.

Willingham, D. (2008). Why Web 2.0 will not be an integral part of K–12 education: A reply to Steve Hargadon. *Encyclopedia Britannica Blog*. Retrieved from www.britannica.com/blogs/2008/10/web-20-will-not-be-the-future-of-k-12-education-a-reply-to-steve-hargadon/.

Wright, N. (2010). Is the digital divide headed in the right direction? *Blackweb 2.0*. Retrieved from www.blackweb20.com/2010/07/21/is-the-digital-divide-headed-in-the-right-direction-lets-be-sure/.

Index

A

AASL. *See* American Association of School Librarians
AASL Standards for 21st-Century Learners, 51
Advertising, 3, 4, 5, 9, 10, 14, 26, 51, 52, 69, 94, 101; and sponsors, 19
AdWords, 3, 14, 101
American Association of School Librarians, 51, 53, 89, 99
Animoto, 21–22, 35, 68, 69, 71
APIs (application programming interfaces), 3
Assessment strategies, 90

B

Barriers, 31, 33, 34, 37, 39, 41, 43, 45, 46, 47, 49, 51, 53, 57, 73, 76, 82–83, 84, 86, 88, 97, 98
Bing, 2, 3–5, 32, 101
Blogs, 1, 7, 12, 16, 17, 18, 20–23, 25, 32, 33, 35, 42, 55, 59, 67, 68, 69, 70, 86, 91, 94, 95, 96, 97, 99, 103, 105, 106, 107
Book Seer, 58
BookTalk, 59
Bookwink, 59–60, 74
Budget cuts, 41–42, 48, 87
Budgets, 39, 42, 43, 78–79

C

Change agents, 87–88; school librarians as, 93–94, 101
Chrome (Google), 2, 3, 4, 5, 6, 17, 32
Cloud computing, 11, 14–16, 101
Clustrmaps, 22, 35, 71
Collaborate, 3, 7, 24, 49, 53, 56, 83, 92, 98
Collaboration, 6, 9, 11, 21, 35, 39, 49, 50, 69, 71, 75, 76, 79, 95, 101, 105, 106, 107; as a 21st-century phenomenon, 11. *See also* Collaborate
Commenting, 11–12, 57, 73. *See also* Comments
Comments, 7, 12, 18, 56, 87, 94–95, 100
Common Core Standards, 89, 100
Consortium for School Networking. *See* CoSN
Constructivist, 6, 48
Copyright infringement, 51, 52
Copyright law, 51, 94
CoSN, 38, 102
Create, 3, 7, 8, 10, 11, 12, 14, 15, 16, 17, 19, 20, 22, 23, 24, 26, 29, 30, 32, 35, 51, 59, 61, 67, 69, 70, 72, 76, 81, 83, 91, 95, 96, 97, 100; a blog, 31; a personal plan, 90, 100; products, 53; a project, 90; value 56; a wiki, 49

Creating, 11, 28, 69–70, 71, 91, 99, 102. *See also* Create
Cyberbullying, 20, 51–52, 54, 102
Cyber theft, 51–52, 102

D

Digital Booktalk, 60–61
Digital divide, 45–49, 51, 54, 102; in schools, 47–49
Digital storytelling, 1, 23, 28, 69, 70, 102
Document sharing, 1, 16, 21, 69, 90, 102
Dynamic, 11, 13–14, 56, 57, 102. *See also* Dynamic code
Dynamic code, 8, 9, 10, 13–14, 32

E

Edublogs, 23, 35, 69
Explorer. *See* Internet Explorer

F

Facebook, 7, 12, 13, 59, 64, 67, 71
Filters, 19–20, 23, 51, 57
Firefox, 2–5, 6, 32
Flickr, 16, 23, 35, 70
Folksonomies, 11, 21

G

Goodreads, 61, 74
Google, 2, 3, 4, 5, 6, 14, 16, 17, 18, 20, 24, 25, 32, 56, 61, 93, 98, 101, 103; Google Advanced Search, 98; Google Books, 62, 74; Google Docs, 16, 24–25, 35, 69; Google Forms, 71; Google LitTrips, 63, 74; Google Maps, 71; Google Scholar, 98; Google Sites, 71–72; Google Voice, 70

H

Hypertext, 2, 13, 19, 102

I

Identity theft, 51
Integrate technology, 41, 54, 76–77, 81, 91, 100
International Children's Digital Library, 63, 74
International Society for Technology in Education, 50, 89
Internet, 2, 5, 6, 7, 12, 14, 15, 16, 17, 18, 19, 20, 21, 24, 29, 38, 40, 46, 47, 51, 54, 56, 86, 102, 103, 104, 106; and cloud computing, 12; filters, 20; web 2.0

architecture, 19. *See also* Internet Explorer
Internet Explorer, 2, 3, 5, 6
Introduction, 2, 3, 16, 71, 106
ISTE, 50, 53, 89, 100. *See also* International Society for Technology in Education

J

Jason Project, 25, 35

L

Lack, 4, 45, 47, 49, 52, 76; of access, 50; of administrative support, 40, 42, 48, 83, 85, 98; of incentives, 77, 81, 83, 86; of technology support, 42, 48, 77, 79, 83, 86; of time, 48, 77–78, 82, 83, 86, 98; of training, 48, 77, 78–79, 86
Lesson plans, 7, 18, 25, 95
Level of technology integration, 89
Library of Congress, 23, 63
LibraryThing, 13, 58, 64, 70, 74

M

Mashing up, 11, 21. *See also* Mashup
Mashup, 21
Media sharing, 11, 18, 21
Michigan, 89
Microblogs, 12, 70, 103
Mozilla, 2–4, 5. *See also* Firefox

N

NASA, 23
National Coordination Office for Networking and Information Technology Research and Development. *See* NITRD
National Educational Technology Standards. *See* NETS
National Geographic, 25
NETS, 50, 53, 100
Netscape, 2, 3, 5
New York State Education Department rubric, 89
New York Times, 6, 19, 107
NITRD, 48–49
NYC Public Library, 23

O

Online Books Page, 65
Open source, 3, 5
Open sourcing, 11

P

Page, Larry, and Sergey Brin, 3
Partnership for 21st Century Skills, 50, 106

PBworks, 26, 35, 72
Photo streams, 1, 100
Podcasts, 1, 65, 67, 68, 74, 78, 106
Podiobooks, 65–66
Positive social change, 53, 75, 83, 88
Prezi, 26–27, 35, 70
Public library, 23, 28, 45, 46

R

Reading Rockets, 66–67, 74
Resource sharing, 1
Richardson, Will, 7, 9, 106
RSS feed, 8, 12, 17, 18, 31, 32, 33, 53, 65, 73, 84, 98, 99. *See also* Syndication

S

Safari, 4, 5, 6
Scholastic Book Wizard, 67
School culture, 43, 44–45, 48, 77, 80–83, 85, 86, 97, 98
School librarians, 12, 26, 31, 33, 37, 51, 55, 57, 58, 68, 72, 73, 74, 75, 83, 84, 87, 88, 89, 90, 93–99; as advocates, 94; as change agents, 93; and classroom teachers, 96; as models, 95; and school culture, 96; and teacher educators, 97; as teacher trainers, 96; as technology trainers, 95; as trend setters, 96
School library, 12, 26, 31, 33, 37, 51, 55, 57, 69, 73, 76, 87, 90, 91, 92, 93, 96
School library media program, 68, 69, 70, 71, 72, 88, 90, 99
School library media specialist, 31, 32, 40, 75, 83
School library 2.0 theory, 53, 55–57, 103
SchoolTube, 27, 35
Search engine. *See* Bing; Google
Sea Research Foundation, 25
Sharing, 1, 7, 9, 11, 12, 14, 16, 18, 19, 21, 25, 29, 56, 57, 69, 71, 87, 90, 91, 96, 98, 102
Smartphones, 12, 46, 93
Smithsonian Institution, 23
Social capital, 56, 103
Socially constructed, 7, 11, 103
Social mapping, 1
Social networking, 8, 9, 10, 12–13, 18, 19, 20, 31, 56, 57, 76, 103
Social networking theory, 56, 103
Spam, 51, 52, 103
Static, 6, 7, 8, 10, 13, 14, 103

Storybird, 28, 35
Story Home, 68, 74
Syndication, 11, 17, 104

T

Tag, 7, 8, 10, 11, 12, 18, 19, 21, 56, 57, 73, 102, 104
Tagging. *See* Tag
Taxonomy, 8, 10, 18, 104
TeacherTube, 29, 35, 41, 96
Tech support. *See* Technology support
Techno revolution, 105
Tchnology integration, 37, 38, 42, 43, 44, 45, 53, 76, 80, 81, 84, 85, 89, 100, 102
Technology support, 41, 42, 48, 73
Technology training, 41, 54, 78, 85, 92, 99
21st century, 11, 23, 28, 34, 41, 50, 51, 61; information literacy, 53, 72; instruction, 32, 53, 88; learners, 51, 57, 72; library media program, 68; school library patrons, 57; school librarians, 55, 83; school library media specialists, 75; schools, 37, 38, 39, 51, 76; services, 57; skills, 40, 50; students, 22, 28, 54, 57; technologies, 58; tools, 88; workforce, 52, 53, 72

U

URL (Universal Resource Locator), 2, 13, 17, 35, 43, 74, 104

V

Vodcasts, 1, 69

W

Web, 1, 2 3, 4, 6, 13, 14, 16, 18, 19, 26, 32, 33, 34, 35, 57, 69, 74, 81, 87, 93, 94, 101, 102, 103, 104, 107
Web browser. *See* Chrome (Google); Firefox; Internet Explorer; Safari
Web 2.0, 1, 2, 6–7, 8, 9, 10, 11, 12, 13, 14, 16, 17, 18, 19, 20, 32, 37, 38, 40, 44, 46, 49, 50, 51, 52, 53, 54, 55, 56, 58, 75, 76, 77, 78, 83, 84, 85, 86, 87, 88, 89, 90, 92, 93, 94, 95, 96, 97, 98, 99, 105, 106, 107; advantages, 49; architecture, 19; barriers to, 37, 83, 86; cloud computing, 14–16; collaboration, 11; defining, 6; disadvantages of, 51–52, 53; dynamic code, 13–14; filtering, 20; folksonomy, 18; media sharing, 18; research on, 76; school library tools, 58–70;

syndication, 17; teaching tools, 21–31, 35; World Wide Web, 2; Web 1.0, 6–10
Widgets, 14, 32, 57
Wikis, 1, 20, 21, 26, 31, 32, 33, 35, 49, 53, 55, 68, 70, 72, 73, 84, 87, 90, 91, 94, 95, 96, 99, 100, 103, 104, 106
Wordle, 16, 30, 35, 72
World Wide Web. *See* World Wide Web Consortium
World Wide Web Consortium, 2

About the Author

PEGGY MILAM CREIGHTON, PhD, is a school librarian, a writer, and a speaker with an interest in educational technology. She has more than 29 years of experience in classroom teaching and library media. She is currently employed as a school library media specialist in Atlanta, Georgia.

Dr. Creighton received her BS in education from Georgia State University, her Master of Early Childhood Education from Mercer University in Atlanta, and her Master of Library Media Education and Instructional Technology from Georgia State University. She earned her EdS in Media and Instructional Technology from the University of West Georgia and achieved her National Board Certification in Library Media the same year. Dr. Creighton earned her PhD in Educational Technology from Walden University. She is active in several professional organizations and is a frequent presenter at conferences. She is also the author of numerous professional articles and two previous books: *National Board Certification in Library Media: A Candidate's Journal* (2005) and *InfoQuest: A New Twist on Information Literacy* (2002), both of which are ABC-CLIO publications.

www.ingramcontent.com/pod-product-compliance
Lightning Source LLC
Chambersburg PA
CBHW070628300426
44113CB00010B/1707